I0071699

THE ENTREPRENEUR'S

BATTLE PLAN

THE ENTREPRENEUR'S BATTLE PLAN

All rights reserved

First Edition, 2021

© Ma Trong Tham, 2021

Publisher: DigiNetStor LLC

No part of this publication may be reproduced, or stored in a retrieval system, or transmitted in any form by means of electronic, mechanical, photocopying or otherwise, without prior written permission from the author.

ISBN 978-1-954891-00-5 (EB)
ISBN 978-1-954891-01-2 (PP)
ISBN 978-1-954891-02-9 (HC)

THE ENTREPRENEUR'S BATTLE PLAN

Winning Strategies For Business

Ma Trong Tham

Contents

INTRODUCTION

It is not a new fact that money sits at the center of everything we do. It may not be mentioned as one of life's necessities like food, shelter, and clothing, but the truth remains that we can only get these necessities through money. Even important intangibles like love and health need money to thrive. It is for this reason that there is an unending quest for financial freedom.

Seeking freedom means that one is held captive by something or someone. And to be free, one either has to be given freedom or fight for freedom. Financial freedom cannot be given. Life does not throw a briefcase of euros on your laps. Life is not that generous. So you *need* to fight to be financially free.

The first step to financial freedom is making your money work for you. There are several ways to do this, like having a business—in other words, entrepreneurship—tops the list.

Entrepreneurship offers independence in key aspects of one's life—time, money, creativity. This independence heightens its allure. But here is the hard truth: The business world is a highly competitive space that is out to swallow your vision and crush you to the ground. It is a battleground. As a businessperson, you'd face stiff opposition from existing businesses that already have a large portion of the market share. You'd face opposition from new businesses who are trying to stamp their presence in the market. You'd face opposition from economic policies and the global economic climate. And ultimately, you'd face opposition from yourself—from that little voice in your head telling you to give up, telling you that it is impossible to surmount the challenges.

Considering the many enemies within and without, you have two choices: back out of the fight, or forge ahead till you gain victory. If you are still reading to this point, it means that you've chosen the latter. Well done. Because you have done this, I will present to you, through this book, working strategies to conquer the business battlefield.

These strategies are based on Sun Vu's *The Law of War*—a book that has guided military strategies and warfare for thousands of years. It is recorded that during his lifetime as a military strategist and general, Vu never lost a battle. He didn't achieve this feat because he had the strongest of soldiers, but because he understood that every battle is unique and, as such, should be approached differently.

Sun Vu and Miyamoto Musashi (whose ideas on military strategy formed the basis for my book, *On The Soldier's Path*) had similar ideologies on warfare. Both men believed that warfare went beyond weapons, so they never followed the conventional paths to warfare. They understood that battles are as mental as they are physical. And for this reason, they developed their own strategies.

A military general in Sun Vu's time would have interpreted battle readiness to mean taking up arms and marching to the battlefield, but for Vu, battle readiness meant having the perfect strategy for each situation. It meant being enigmatic, unpredictable. It was a principle that led to countless victories, not just for him but for generals after him that depended on his principle.

Dear reader, see yourself as a soldier, only that you are fighting a financial war—a fight for your freedom. And here is an exciting fact: you will win this war because you have this book in your hands.

The Entrepreneur's Battle Plan is a step-by-step guide for navigating the rigorous terrain of the business world. It is a journey that begins from you getting it right at The Drawing Board (Chapter One) and terminates at how to use spies to win in the business battlefield (Chapter Ten). Between the start and endpoint lie several tactics (e.g., unpredictable maneuvering), resources (e.g., having a winning team), and qualities (e.g., resilience) you must possess to come out victorious. Each chapter of this book is summed up with words of affirmation. These words of affirmation will inspire you to take action. It is not enough furnishing you with strategies for business; it is important you take action. Taking action begins with getting your mind ready and unburdened from any limitation or doubt. And this is what each chapter will help you do.

The victor or vanquished is never known before a battle. But by having this book in your hands, you know you are coming out of the Business Battlefield a victor. Sun Vu's strategies worked for him and those after him. And it is on this knowledge that you should build your trust, knowing that you will win. With this in mind, let's march to the battlefield.

CHAPTER ONE

The Drawing Board

"Give me six hours to chop down a tree, and I will spend the first four sharpening the ax."

— Abraham Lincoln

Many have an unintentional approach to business. For them, business is more of an escape route than it is about offering value and solving a need. By a stroke of luck, some have been successful with this approach, but for others, it has backfired. A lot of people go into business as a last resort. They are unemployed; they start a business. The economy is bad; they start a business. They hear that a particular industry is booming; they start a business. In countries in Africa, for instance, youths are advised to go into business as a way of being gainfully employed since their governments have failed them. While this may be a logical reason for starting a business, it has made many jump the gun and venture into businesses that at their worst, lack a solid foundation, or at their best, subsistent.

The first step towards starting a business is to have a plan. Every step in your business should be mapped. This is not to say you must get everything figured out at once. Plans and visions are bound to evolve, but before they do, you must have them first.

Sun Vu stated that there are five determinants that a soldier must plan towards during a war. They are Righteousness, Atmosphere, Terrain, General, and Martial Law.

Righteousness

About righteousness, Sun Vu wrote: *Righteousness is a way of making people willing to join with the king, to make them unite and join forces, to live and die with courage.*

The popular mantra is that the customer is king. Others even say that cash is king. These positions are understandable, but the ultimate truth is that in business, you—the entrepreneur—is king. You navigate the ship of the business. Your failure to navigate the ship as you ought to would lead to its capsize.

Now that you know you are king, the question you should ask is: *Why should people join forces with me?* These forces can be categorized into two: your team and your customers. The bulk of the work starts with getting the right team. If you can get the right team that buys into your vision, getting the customers would be easy.

Your Team

One thing you should know is that your vision is so big for you to fulfill alone. Think about behemoth companies—Microsoft, Apple, Amazon, Facebook, Alphabet, Tencent, Walmart, etc. Do you think they would have been global brands if their owners had decided to build alone? That would have been impossible.

Human resources are the greatest resource on earth. Although it is a resource that is difficult to control, it plays a vital role in any business. Your team does not only consist of your employees, it includes your investors and partners as well; it includes anyone who plays a role in your business. Your business, even if it is a startup, is a chain. And a chain is only as strong as its weakest link.

Know this: Humans are soils. Humans can take in your vision, nourish it, and make it grow. Before you make people willing to join you, you must first understand that just like there are different soil types for farming, humans can also be categorized by soil types. There are sandy humans and loamy humans. You should know the features of each category so that you can spot them and know which to utilize and which to avoid. Everyone shouldn't be on your team. Selecting the wrong soil as part of your team may be the beginning of the end of your business.

The Sandy Humans

Sandy soil is light, warm, acidic, and low in nutrients. Drains water easily. Nutrients are easily washed away by rain.[1]

Sandy humans have all the qualities of sandy soil.

1. Light: In terms of soil texture, heavy soil has a high proportion of clay, while light soil has more sand than clay.[2] Heavy soil, although hard to till because of the *stickiness* of clay, is more fertile than light soil.[3]

Sandy humans are not fertile. They can easily kill a vision. They do not have the patience or the capacity to *stick* with you till your vision starts to yield fruit. In this case, clay is a symbol of loyalty, faithfulness, and dedication to you and your cause. Sandy humans lack these qualities. They are light; they have no substance. The essence of building a team is to have people who can enhance and spread your vision. Sandy humans cannot do this. They contribute nothing to the growth of your vision.

2. Warm and drains water easily: Water is life. It is needed for the growth and sustenance of every living thing. Therefore, a soil must have a good moisture-retention capacity. The moisture content in a soil also helps reduce its temperature. Unless it is in a plant's nature to thrive in high temperatures, all plants will die if the soil's temperature is high.

Here, water is a metaphor for passion. Every business needs passion for success. Passion pushes you to become better, to never give up. But sandy humans lack this vital quality. They lack drive. They easily lose their passion and enthusiasm for the vision.

Asides passion, water also represents encouragement, the voice of reason. Running a business can be overwhelming, especially in the business's budding phase. This is why it is necessary to have people who wouldn't add to the heat of running the business, people who will encourage you to strive harder, people who will soothe you in times of distress, people who will be your voice of reason in times when you think giving up is the best and only option. Sandy humans aren't these people. They lose passion easily, so they can't encourage you to keep up with a vision they do not believe in. Sandy humans add to the heat of running your business. Your business cannot thrive with their presence.

3. Acidic: Acids are toxic. They corrode whatever they come in contact with. They stunt the growth of plants. Sandy humans are usually toxic. They possess qualities (e.g., rudeness, carelessness, greed) that are unhealthy for a business. Many business owners underestimate the value of character when recruiting employees. They focus on skill and experience, relegating character to the background. But skill and experience are not enough to maintain consistent patronage.

Human beings are emotional species. They have a sense of worth. No one will continuously patronize a business where they are disrespected or where their rights are trampled on. Sandy humans have toxic traits and attitudes that are capable of sending your customers away. Thus, you need to know the kind of people you bring to be part of your vision. As the business owner, you may have all the traits required to keep the customer happy, but you cannot attend to every customer at every time.

For this reason, you need the *right* people to attend to the customers just as you would have. And sandy humans are not the right hands for the job.

4. <u>Nutrients are easily washed by rain</u>: Recall that sandy soils have low amounts of clay, so they cannot retain or hold moisture and nutrients. Sandy soils are loose soils, and the little nutrients that can be found in them are easily washed off by rain.

Sandy humans lack resilience. They lack staying capacity. You may think that they love and want to be part of your vision all the way, but when the rains come, they lose their integrity and loyalty. When the storms of the business world hit (e.g., economic recession, unfavorable policies, inflation, stiff competition), sandy humans will be revealed for who they are—people without substance.

Nutrients are also a metaphor for ideas. You can only expand your vision as an entrepreneur through ideas. Your team, apart from being employees and investors, should be your think-tank. They have seen and imbibed your vision. Thus, it is only rational that they come up with key ideas that would grow the vision. Sandy humans lack ideas, and in cases where they do have ideas, their ideas do not stand the test of time. Why? They do not think in the long term.

By their nature, sandy humans are impatient and are only interested in quick gains. As mentioned earlier, they lack resilience and staying capacity. So their suggestions for your company would only be focused on what can bring quick, small gains today, and not what will bring huge profits tomorrow, albeit slowly.

If you make the mistake of implementing their idea, you will discover that it won't stand the test of time. If you are unlucky, it may destroy all you've built.

The Loamy Humans

Loamy soil is rich in nutrients. It has high water-retention capacity because it contains a significant proportion of clay. It can also drain water easily. It is easy to till.[4]

So, who are loamy humans?

1. <u>They are heavy with nutrients</u>: They are resourceful people. They are a hotbed of ideas. They understand and accept your vision. They have ideas to push and expand your vision. Just tell it to them, and they run along with it as if the vision is their personal project. They contain clay—they are loyal and dedicated. They have staying capacity. They are there through the thick and thin of your business.

Plant your vision in their hearts and watch it grow.

2. <u>Retains water</u>: Their passion never dies. They are committed to your cause. All they desire is to watch your vision expand. They are there to calm you down when the going gets tough.

3. <u>Easy to till</u>: These people understand that you are in the driving seat, so they are willing to follow your lead at all times. They are independent and smart enough not to be micromanaged, yet loyal enough to flow in your direction. Some people would want to take over your business because they feel they are indispensable. You would encounter challenges when you have such people in your team. Loamy humans do not think they are indispensable. They do not put you in a position where you would have to choose between working with them and saving your business. They treat your vision as theirs and wouldn't do anything to jeopardize it.

Your business would thrive in the presence of loamy humans.

Now that you know the qualities of sandy and loamy humans, the next step would be to know how to spot these people.

Spotting sandy or loamy humans may be quite difficult because it takes time for an individual's true character to be revealed. However, I believe that the best way to know a person's character or value is to listen to what they say when they are not under duress. Listen to their comments on social, financial, or business issues, then you would be able to tell their character.

In the next chapter, I will outline the steps to follow to spot sandy or loamy before selecting your team.

To expand your business, you must be able to plant your vision in the hearts of others. It is an important step. Once you can do this correctly, then it would be easy to move on to the next determinant—atmosphere.

Atmosphere

Sun Vu wrote: *Atmosphere is night or day, hotness and coldness, and change of four seasons.*

As an entrepreneur, you have to be discerning of seasons. A business is built to evolve and those who will profit from it are those who understand seasons.   Many companies are fettered by mediocrity because they cannot comprehend seasons and/or tailor their activities according to seasons.

The Four Business Seasons

Just like the earth has four seasons, there are four seasons in business: spring, summer, autumn, and winter. Peter Brodie, a member of Forbes Council, described the four seasons thus: "In spring, you build business plans, create new services and products, and design new marketing materials.   In summer, everything is in full swing.   You're busy supporting existing clients, and you continue to promote your services to attract a growing list of new ones.   In autumn, the pace of work slows.   You still have a core list of clients, but your services and promotional materials grow tired and jaded.   Then, in winter, the cold settles in, with no growth or new clients in sight. You're dependent on what you've stored away in preparation for this bleak time."[5]

What you do at each season of your business determines how successful you would become. These four seasons are important and they all have their use—including the autumn and winter seasons.

As a new entrepreneur, the first season you enter is the spring season. Here, you are bubbling with ideas and passion. You make plans, draft strategies, and implement these strategies. You create. You build. You grow. If you get the spring season right, then you would have an exciting summer.

In summer, you watch everything you've planted yield fruits. You consolidate your work with more promotions, more investments, and more innovations. But this phase is not meant to last forever because autumn is just by the corner.

In autumn, there seems to be a tapering of success. It may seem as though you are fastened to a spot. There is no enthusiasm from your clients. Business slows down. The numbers aren't as high as they were before. And just when you are trying to overcome autumn, it starts to snow. Winter has come.

Winter comes with a pause. A biting cold. A depressing phase. No new clients. No innovation. No development. No increase in the numbers. And there is nothing you can do about it.

You must understand these seasons so you wouldn't channel your energy to the wrong activity. The spring season is not a time to rest; it is a period to sow. A season of implementation. A season of action. It is the season where you make the right connections. It is the season to get people into your team. Create and test new products. Improve your customer service. It is not a time to relax. Usually, the spring season is exciting—you are exhausted by all the work, yet you are thrilled by what you are building.

The result of your hard work during the spring season will be revealed in summer. Mind you, not every seed that was sown would germinate and yield fruits. This is why the summer season is important. It is a time to assess yourself. What did you get right? What did you do wrongly? How do you improve and scale up what you did right? What approach would you use to correct your mistakes? Summer is not just a time to enjoy the bubbles of success, it is also a time to reflect on how to consolidate this success. It is easy to get carried away with the warmth of summer and not notice when autumn begins to creep in.

With conventional weather, autumn marks the transition from summer to winter. Nature knows that it would be too sudden to switch between two temperature extremes with no warning, so autumn is that season that prepares us for winter. Similarly, the autumn season of business is meant to prepare you for what lies ahead in winter. Once the decline starts happening, once you stop seeing the bubbles, it means it is time to prepare yourself mentally and financially for winter. Don't allow yourself to be caught unawares.

Winter may be a cold and depressing period, but it is a time of evaluation. Don't lose track of your vision because you feel things are not the way they should be. The winter season is the time to brainstorm and think out new ideas. It is a time to relax with your team and evaluate the next step to take. The ideas you birth during winter are the ideas that you would implement during spring.

Every season is important. And in the world of business, the winter season of one businessperson may be the summer season of another. Peter Brodie put it rightly when he pointed out that there are neither winners nor losers in the business world; there are only seasons to be enjoyed.[6] The business world is an interplay of individual seasons. The period where you are winning and recording huge success is the same period another is at a consistent loss. There is no way to eradicate autumn and winter, leaving only spring and summer. Brodie stated that "most service professionals would like to make the warm, busy days of summer last forever. But too much sun and heat—too much work—will dry things up and create cracks. Both you and your business need periods of rest. You must give way to autumn to recover from the summer frenzy."

These seasons do not have definite lengths. But as an entrepreneur, your goal should be to have longer summers and shorter winters. "The duration is determined by the quality of work you invest into the business during spring. If you take the time to plant and propagate healthy seeds, you'll have long summers and short winters."[7]

Trends

Another aspect of atmosphere you must be able to discern as a businessperson is trends. Sometimes the seasons of your business are determined by the general trends of the market. Just as your business is bound to evolve, the market or industry is also bound to evolve. I have categorized business trends into five types: Uptrend, Downtrend, Sideways, Fads, and Disruption. Every market or industry reflects one or more of these trends from time to time.

Uptrend

This is the period in the market or industry where the value of products is consistently rising due to the high demand for the products. During this period, vendors make huge revenues. The upward trend coincides with the summer season of many entrepreneurs.

For instance, the online education industry experienced a boom during the heat of the coronavirus pandemic. There was massive adoption of online education during the lockdown. Many schools and individuals had to fully adopt online learning to keep up with their curriculum. For instance, when the Chinese government instructed 250 million full-time students to resume their studies through online learning, it resulted in what was dubbed the largest "online movement" in the history of online education as about 730,000 (that is, 81 percent of K-12) students attended classes online through the Tencent K-12 Online School in Wuhan.[8]

The World Economic Forum states that even before the coronavirus pandemic, there has been a massive adoption of online education worldwide. Global edtech investments reached 18.66 billion USD in 2019, and the overall market for online education was projected to reach 350 billion USD by 2025.[9]

With reports like this, entrepreneurs in the industry can accurately position themselves to have a significant market share before the uptrend stops. Other industries that experienced an upward trend due to the coronavirus pandemic include lifestyle of health and sustainability and wellness, delivery/logistics services, remote work, and entertainment industries.[10]

Downtrend

As you already know, this is the opposite of an upward trend. During a downtrend, an industry experiences a steady decline in value. Due to some political or economic factors, the interest of people towards an industry may dwindle. The downward trend coincides with the winter of many entrepreneurs.

An example of an industry that has experienced a downward trend is the global airline industry. Although the industry witnesses a rise in passenger and cargo traffic, it has been steadily declining because of volatile fuel prices and steady competition in the last five years. Between 2019 and 2020, it had revenue growth of -12.8 percent. This decline worsened with the coronavirus pandemic.[11] Richard Branson's Virgin Atlantic had to file for bankruptcy protection four months after Virgin Australia went into administration, owing 6.8 billion USD to over 12,000 creditors.[12]

A downtrend does not always translate to a total collapse of an industry. It is often a temporary setback—a pullback—so that the industry can regenerate itself. Some entrepreneurs and investors see downtrends as the perfect opportunity to make more investments. For instance, when many investors were trying to protect their investments because of the pandemic (I write of the pandemic because it is the most significant factor that impacted every industry around the world), the Oracle of Omaha, Warren Buffett invested 6 billion USD in five of Japan's biggest trading companies.[13]

Sideways

This is a term popular in finance industries like the stock market, forex, and cryptocurrency. But it can apply to other industries or sectors. In a sideways trend, the market neither moves up or down. Supply and demand for products in the industry are equal. Sideways trend precedes an uptrend or a downtrend. It is also known as consolidation because investors hold on to their assets since they don't know the direction the market would take.[14]

It suffices to say that a sideways trend that precedes an uptrend will coincide with the entrepreneur's spring season, while a sideways trend that precedes a downtrend will coincide with autumn.

Fads

We can describe a fad as a short-lived trend. A fad storms a market or industry, creates a buzz, and fades away as quickly as it came. Most times, fads are not genuine. For instance, between 2016 and 2017, the cryptocurrency industry was agog with the fake currency called OneCoin. It was dubbed "The Bitcoin Killer." Ruja Ignatova, the lady behind the project, called herself the Cryptoqueen and persuaded people to invest in her crypto project which would rival Bitcoin. But it was only a Ponzi scheme. The so-called digital asset was not on the blockchain—the technology that backs cryptocurrency assets. Dr. Ignatova made $4 billion selling a fake cryptocurrency to the world, then disappeared without a trace.[15] And the fad ended.

At other times, fads may be genuine but lack the tenacity to remain and compete in the market for a long time. An example of a genuine fad is Pokemon Go—a gaming app that made waves in 2016. Although it is reported that the gaming app had a record year in 2019, raking about $900 million through in-app purchases,[16] its 2016 buzz was gone.

It is difficult to predict what is a fad and what is not. Some products have been classed as fads and they ended up being staple products. An example is Twitter. Between 2009 and 2010, many questioned if the microblogging app had perpetuity or if it was another fad.[17, 18] In 2013, a blogger even described the app as an internet force—"a force. . . for 140 characters worth of banal nonsense."[19] But can those words still be used to describe the app with a current market capitalization of over $37 billion?

The greatest innovation ever known to humankind was also classified as a fad. In 1995, Clifford Stoll, a technologist author and columnist for Newsweek claimed that the internet would never work and would die after 1996.[20] I don't need to write about the outcome of that prediction. The internet was never a fad; it was a disruption.

Disruption

Merriam-Webster Dictionary defines disruption as a break or interruption in the normal course or continuation of some activity, process, etc.[21] Therefore, a disruption is more than a trend or a fad; it is a new way of life.

In his insightful *Forbes* article, Caroline Howard stated that disruption uproots and changes how we think, behave, do business, learn and go about our day-to-day. Quoting Clayton Christensen, a Harvard Business School professor, Howard explained that a disruption "displaces an existing market, industry, or technology and produces something new and more efficient and worthwhile. It is at once destructive and creative."[22]

Every disruption begins as a new trend, and sometimes, they get labeled as fads. We saw earlier how there was a prediction that the internet wouldn't survive, but more than two decades later, it has become the fulcrum for our every activity. The internet disrupted and replaced analog methods of doing things. Some people have missed huge financial opportunities because they were unable to spot and take advantage of disruptions. In 2010, a young man attempted to auction off 10,000 bitcoins for $50. No one knew if he succeeded or if he had a rethink and retained the digital asset. If we assume he sold off all his bitcoins, that means he auctioned off his opportunity to become about 180 million dollars richer ten years later. The blockchain and cryptocurrency industry is disrupting and revolutionizing global financial systems as we know them. With cryptocurrency, people can now actually have money as a store of value. Although the industry has been in existence for 10-11 years, it is still a budding industry when compared to the stock market and Forex. The New York Stock Exchange (NYSE) had a market capitalization of $25 trillion as of April 2020.[23] Forex has a market capitalization of around $5.1 trillion.[24] However, the cryptocurrency market is just a little over $758 billion as at 2020.[25] Smart entrepreneurs and investors are getting on this disruptive train before becoming saturated in the nearest future.

Jeff Bezos was a man who recognized a disruption and took advantage of it. He decided to take advanatge of the web after reading, in 1994, that the web had grown 2300 percent in one year. He made a list of 20 products he could sell online, and settled for books. The information on the internet then was less than 1 percent of the wealth of information available today. Yet, Bezos believed in the future of the internet. He left the hedge fund company, D. E. Shaw, where he had risen to vice-president to start his company: Amazon.[26] That singular belief in the internet—a disruption—has made Jeff Bezos the richest man in the world today.

Your ability as an entrepreneur to recognize and understand the atmosphere (seasons and trends) you are in would determine how well you would navigate your terrain. It is just like a physical journey. A road may be rough or the sky may be bumpy with clouds, but the journey becomes even more difficult and hazardous if the atmosphere is unfavorable.

Terrain

Geographically, terrain has to do with an area of land and its physical features. Nayturr.com defined terrain as the earth's horizontal and vertical surfaces. By identifying the different types of terrain, we can determine the most suitable habitats for humankind. The site listed 14 types of terrain, namely: canyon, desert, forest, glacier, hill, marsh, mountain, oasis, ocean, open, river, swamp, tundra, and valley.[27]

Just like identifying terrains can help us determine the suitable habitat for humankind, identifying business terrains can help you determine where and how to pitch your business. In this book, I will use some geographical terrains as allegories for business terrains. Thus, there are three types of terrains in business: canyon/valley, desert/oasis, and forest.

Forest

A forest is an area of land completely covered with vegetation—grasses and trees. Forest trees are perennial and survive for a long time. New trees would have to go through the process of growing as tall as the old trees. And to do this, they would need to compete for resources with the old trees. It would take a resilient tree to survive and grow as it should.

What does this mean in business?

In business, the forest is the commonest terrain. It is a terrain where there are multiple businesses, a terrain of stiff competition. An entrepreneur in this terrain would have to strive hard to stand tall above other trees or, at least, be on the same level with them. Except there is an innovative side to your business, it is unprofitable to be in this terrain because it is often saturated.

Desert/Oasis

A desert is a large, often hot, and dry piece of land with little or no vegetation due to factors like lack of water, bad soil, or salt poisoning. Most often than not, there is no water source in a desert. However, there are cases where there is an isolated area in a desert surrounded by a water source such as a spring, pond, or small lake. Such an area is known as an oasis.

Your business can be an oasis in a desert. You can venture into areas that others see as dry and unfavorable. The desert/oasis is often the toughest terrain, but its returns are huge *if* it eventually pays off. This was the story of Elon Musk's Tesla and SpaceX, especially the latter. A lot of people believed that it is ridiculous to venture into rockets. For them, rockets were the exclusive preserve of huge government organizations.[28] Yet, it was in this supposed desert that Musk decided to be an oasis. Today, he is the second richest man in the world.

Being an oasis in the desert requires taking calculated risks. It requires playing in a field where others have not played before. Thus you need to count the cost before venturing into the business. Elon Musk's idea almost crashed. SpaceX had three launch failures. If the fourth launch had failed, then that would have been it for the company. Yet, Musk believed in his idea and was funding it from his personal money. At a point, he had to sell his car.[29]

If you believe in the validity of your vision, you can aim to be an oasis in the desert.

Canyon/Valley

A canyon is a big gorge in the ground found between escarpments or cliffs *due to erosion from a river or other weather conditions.* A canyon is similar to a valley—a low area between mountains or hills with a river flowing through it. By geographical definition, canyons are formed due to erosion. This means that they were not hitherto present but were created over time due to atmospheric conditions.

What does this mean for an entrepreneur?

Some businesses or industries spring up or expand due to a drastic change in the economic climate. For instance, after 9/11, experts and researchers began investigating methods for improved surveillance technology. Technologies considered include remote-controlled airliners, bio-monitors, remote video monitoring, light guns, superthin flexible body armor, and missile disrupters.[30]

Another example is the explosion of certain industries due to the coronavirus pandemic. Telemedicine, pharmaceutical, online education, e-commerce, online payment, and delivery industries all recorded massive growth due to the pandemic. Just like erosion or adverse weather conditions create a canyon, the pandemic created canyons of businesses.

What this tells us is that entrepreneurs should always seek the positives within adversities. Seeking the positives in adversities is an indicator of a high adversity quotient. In adversity lies a lot of business opportunities. Adversities often reveal new problems; these problems would require solutions. And that's where you come in as a businessperson. Ask yourself: How can I offer value amid these challenges? What solution can I provide? How can I be a canyon?

General

As mentioned earlier, you are king, you are the leader. You are the magnet that attracts every other person to your vision. You are the commander. The general. Because of this, there are qualities you must possess. You must be strategic, trustworthy, kind, courageous, and strict/firm. Your team should possess these qualities too, but they can only do so if you show them the way. When your business expands, you'd have team leads who would oversee different aspects of your company. They can only carry out their leadership function if they see and act as generals. But first, they must learn and imitate the chief general: you.

Strategic

Entrepreneurs have to understand the atmosphere and terrain so that they can be strategic. No general goes to war without a battle plan, a strategy. Going to war without a strategy is suicide. While there are things you'd still have to learn through experience, a business without a clearly defined plan would fail. There is no guesswork in business. Every action taken must be a product of purposeful thought and a documented plan.

Members of your team should know your strategy and the roles they have to play. Divide your vision into short-term, mid-term, and long-term goals. The accumulation and attainment of these goals will lead to the overall success of your vision.

Have the right strategy for you cannot go wrong with one.

Trustworthy

One factor that limits new brands from competing favorably with established brands is trust. Over the years, big brands have created value and gotten their customers to *trust* that they would always deliver. For this reason, a new Samsung phone or iPhone or PlayStation 5 can get sold out within hours to days of release. People are ready to be among the first buyers because they trust the company launching the product.

Before people can trust your product, you need to be trustworthy first. Many businesses do not survive because they were started and maintained by cutting corners. They offer substandard products, claiming that their products are the best. Customers buy the products, use them, and discover they've been scammed. Since no one gets a second chance to create a first impression, the business begins to die.

Trust is a vital attribute needed for the success of a business. Neil Patel stated that trust is the foundation of strong business relationships, and entrepreneurs with a high level of trust are more successful at retaining employees.[31] This means that one fundamental way to have the right team is to be trustworthy. Patel further stated that to build trust, an entrepreneur must first see it as a priority.

Kind

Your products or services aren't offered to machines but human beings. Thus, you have to be kind when dealing with people—both employees and customers. Many entrepreneurs are so focused on their business that they have lost every sense of empathy and kindness. The only language they understand is money. This is a wrong approach to business. It is one of the dangerous drawbacks that can destroy a business. We will see this later.

Do not lose your humanity because you are an entrepreneur. Running a business can indeed be daunting, but you must not miss the opportunity of forging and sustaining human connections. Recognize the worth of humans and make sure you do not diminish their worth.

It is important to note that being kind does not translate to turning your business into a charity organization. Being a people pleaser is another dangerous drawback to a business. You have to maintain your business's image and worth without losing the qualities that make you human. Use your discretion to strike a balance.

Courageous

By starting a business, you have already displayed immense courage. Never lose this courage. The business world is a den of hungry lions ready to devour you as soon as you step into it. One needs to be courageous to be able to maneuver the challenges and come out strong. Without courage, you would be unable to apply the strategies you've mapped out. The lack of courage is a syndrome that can cripple a business. Four signs accompany lack of courage: doubt, fear, discouragement, and quitting. These signs follow an order and creep up as questions. Once you don't nip them in the bud early enough, your transition from doubt to quitting would be swift.

- Doubt: Am I sure this strategy would work?

- Fear: Am I sure nothing would go wrong if I apply this strategy?

- Discouragement: Am I sure I can compete with the top players in the industry?

- Quitting: Am I sure this is what I should be doing?

As an entrepreneur, these questions would pop in your mind once in a while, but "no" should never be your answer. Always say, "yes." Be positive. Let your positivity refuel your courage. Let it remind you why you are on the journey in the first place. Let it remind you that you can win.

Strict/Firm

Sun Vu required the general to be strict, but I think "firmness" should be a better word. Being strict is being a wood—rigid, unyielding, unwilling to adapt to change, losing touch with one's emotion. On the other hand, being firm is being a metal—strong, stable, resolute, malleable.

As a business person, you have to be firm, else you'd be taken for granted. Your team and customers should know and understand your place as the boss, the custodian of the vision.

Let them know that you are open to ideas provided that these ideas are in line with the company's culture and vision. Never lose your humanity, but draw the line between business and pleasure.

This is one of the challenges people who have remote workers face. Remote workers often feel that working remotely means eating your cake and having it. That is, they get paid monthly for a job while they live like they are on vacation. An entrepreneur that faces such a challenge should be firm and let the workers know that order *must* be maintained at *all* times.

People are most likely to disregard the order of a leader who is not firm in running an organization. Firmness is one true way of gaining respect. The people know that you respect and value their human worth, but you are not ready to sacrifice your company's success on the altar of laxity.

Martial Law

Sun Vu wrote that martial law refers to the organization and management of soldiers and military expenditure.

Organization and management are the principal duty of an entrepreneur. This is why many entrepreneurs bear the title "Chief Executive Officer" or "Managing Director." Even though the company has different experts handling a company's technical and financial aspects, the entrepreneur still has to oversee, organize, and manage them.

You don't need to be a techie or financial guru before you can oversee the financial aspects of your company. Brian Chesky, the co-founder and CEO of Airbnb, oversees an tech company, yet he has no tech background. He created Airbnb by hiring those who could handle the tech aspects of the company. Not being a tech guru didn't mean he would cede the company's organizational and managerial control to the tech experts. As long as Airbnb is concerned, Brian Chesky (alongside the other two co-founders) is the brain behind its success. He had a vision, knew what he wanted, and found people who could bring that vision to life. Even if he steps down as CEO, the new CEO would run the company using the template Brian had put in place.

The entrepreneur has the job of overseeing every aspect of the company, whether they are knowledgeable in the field or not. This is why Vu said that in martial law, a general not only manages soldiers, but also the *expenditure* of the military. A general is a man of war and strategy, yet he has the duty to manage the military finances. This does not mean he would take up an accountant's job, it only means that he has the prerogative of stating how funds would be disbursed.

This is the same for the entrepreneur. See yourself as a soccer coach. Not all soccer coaches know how to play soccer. Their forte is team management and tactics. You are just like them. So get a team. Hire accountants, tech gurus, marketing personnel, graphic designers, social media experts, and so on. But always remember that how these different professionals carry out their duties depends largely on your directives.

Pledge to Action

I affirm that:

I believe in the validity of my vision.

I believe I can meet a need in the world with it.

As a result, I will attract the right people to me.

I will attract people that will stick with me and grow with me.

I will navigate the harsh seasons and tough terrains.

I understand that tough seasons do not last.

So I know I will enjoy the blissful moments of summer.

I have the eyes of an eagle to spot uptrends and disruptions.

I am ready to take advantage of these trends and win.

I will be the general who is strategic, trustworthy, kind, courageous, and firm.

I let go off fear, doubt, discouragement, and quitting.

I am ready to launch my vision.

So here I am at the drawing board.

CHAPTER TWO

The Attack

"Without a plan, there's no attack. Without attack, no victory."

— Curtis Armstrong

The planning phase is the most important phase in starting a business, but if you fail to launch, your plan becomes only a dormant, documented dream. The dictionary defines attack as "to set *work* upon a task or problem." The attacking phase is the work phase. Sun Vu called it the combat phase. At this phase, you test the strength of your vision, the viability of your ideas.

Sun Vu stated that during combat, the general recruits his soldiers and makes provision for expenses such as food, weapons, repairs, etc. During combat, you breathe life to everything you had documented in your plan. By attacking, you will be giving flesh to the five determinants—Righteousness, Atmosphere, Terrain, General, and Martial Law—you considered at the drawing board.

I have already explained how to attack three of the five determinants namely: Terrain, General, and Martial Law. So in this chapter, we will be focusing on the first two determinants—Righteousness and Atmosphere.

Righteousness

According to Sun Vu, righteousness is all about inspiring others to believe in your vision and join hands with you to bring it to fruition. In the previous chapter, we saw that human beings are soils, and just like there are different soils on the earth, there are different human soils. Now that you know the characteristics of sandy and loamy humans, the next step is how to recruit the best soil for your business.

Sun Vu noted that a general who knows how to use soldiers would not have to recruit soldiers twice.

In business, continuous recruitment is necessary to fill in gaps and meet company needs, however, when you manage your team effectively, you will have people who will stick with you for the long haul. So how do you select your team as a budding entrepreneur?

Steps to follow for team selection (How to spot human soil types)

- Do not rush into recruitment immediately. By recruitment, I mean conducting interviews and employing staff to begin their duty immediately. I know this contradicts what is currently obtainable because if you don't recruit, how do you get people to work with you? The answer lies in the next step.

- Get a group of people and present your vision to them. These people may be your family, friends, colleagues, and so on. Gather them together and share what you have in mind with them. Do not attach any reward to your vision. Do not entice people into working with you. Only present to them your roadmap and allow them make their choice.

As a startup, you have the opportunity of interacting with people and telling them about what you have in mind. Ask them if they would want to come on board. You would be at peace knowing that someone is working with you because they believe in what you do and not because they expect to be paid.

Don't get me wrong—payment is necessary. Money is motivation. But many people want to receive payment without offering value. And the only way to offer value is by understanding the vision of a business and aligning every action to this vision.

- After you have gathered these people, observe them. The sandy or loamy traits of individuals are often revealed with time. Thus, you have to pay attention to the little things and the big things your team members do. You can know sandy or loamy people through the questions they ask. Sandy people ask questions or say things like:

   - What will I benefit from this?

   - Why is it taking so long to see results?

   - Are you sure we aren't wasting time with this vision?

   - I am not sure I can handle this; you'd have to go through this alone.

   - Let's take what we can get now. We don't know tomorrow.

The last point may seem logical, but if the founders of Silicon Valley companies had taken only what they could get at the beginning of their business where would they have been now?

Loamy people think long term and ask questions or say things like:

   - How will this benefit the company in the long term?

   - Does the action align with the vision of the company?

   - I know it is tough, but we have to keep pushing on.

   - Let's appreciate the little wins of today because they are pointers to what tomorrow holds for us.

- Spotting loamy individuals does not automatically mean they would be part of your team. There is a vital quality you must look out for in them: passion. You may ask: "If loamy humans are not passionate, how come they ask questions or make statements like the ones outlined above?" Indeed, those statements or questions spell passion, but are the individuals passionate about *your* business. A person can have all the characteristics of a loamy soil, yet they may not be passionate about your vision. Your prospective team members reserve the prerogative to choose or determine where they would flourish in their personal, career, and financial development.

If a person feels that your vision or business would limit their growth, they may not be passionate about it. For instance, a person who has a flair for fashion may not devote to your real estate company. Put them in your company and they would only be forced to work. It is not that they do not believe in your vision or its viability; they just have an interest in a different vision.

Steve Jobs understood how important passion is, that's why it was the fundamental requirement he looked out for when recruiting. He search for passion was spurred by an experience he had. In the early days of Apple, Jobs had hired two managers to be part of his journey to building a successful company. It was a wrong move. Jobs had to fire them. He called them bozos who knew how to manage but didn't know how to do anything. After that experience, Jobs went for people who knew their opinions and had the passion to flow with the company's vision. He said that he "wanted people that were insanely great at what they did, but were not necessarily those seasoned professionals, but who had at the tips of their fingers and in their passion the latest understanding of where technology was and what they could do with that technology."[1]

Passion, most times, trumps qualifications. A passionate worker will strive to imbibe any skill that will make him an asset to himself, to you, and to your company. But a skillful worker bereft of passion is useless to you. In fact, such a person becomes a liability—slowing you down, drawing you back to levels you should have superseded. It was this for reason, Jobs did not care about the resume of his employees; all he wanted were passionate problem solvers. He found one in Debi Coleman, an inexperienced 32-year-old lady who had a degree in English Literature. Jobs used her to replace the managers he had fired. She worked as Apple's manufacturing chief, and in three years, she became the company's CFO.[2]

A passionate employee doesn't need to be managed. He or she knows what the company is all about and takes initiative that will fulfil the company's goals and objectives. For Jobs, great employees should not be managed. He explained that so long as the employees are *passionate*, smart, and motivated, they would manage themselves. Jobs didn't hire people who he would teach their jobs, he hired those whom he could share his vision and they would work towards the same goal. Apple had a litmus test for spotting such people: they would show the interviewee the Macintosh prototype. If the interviewee's eyes did not light up, if they were not excited, then they didn't belong with Apple.[3]

- When you have successfully spotted and separated the sandy and the loamy team members, and found the ones passionate about your vision, then you can now proceed on your entrepreneurial journey.

The need to have the right team cannot be overemphasized. Bill Gates stated that the ability to build a team is one of his superpowers. Building a team is a skill Gates developed over time as he built Microsoft. He said that it usually took five to six years to assemble *teams* of engineers, alongside understanding what works and what does not. For Gates, it was a game of patience. That skill he developed more than forty years ago has come in handy in these times. In his quest to eradicate global issues like malnutrition and poverty, and diseases like malaria and HIV/AIDS, Gates and his wife, Melinda have had to build and oversee teams of researchers, strategists, and other partners. Gates Foundation has about 1,500 employees around the world.[4] It is with these teams that he had saved the lives of 122 million children by accelerating vaccines getting to children to prevent diseases like pneumococcus and rotavirus[5]; it is with these teams that he had reduced malaria cases and mortality by 40% and 60% respectively[6]; and it is with these teams that he aimed to prevent more than 11 million deaths, 3.9 million disabilities, and 264 million illnesses by 2020[7].

It is not just about having a team but having the right team. In an article for American Express, Donna Fenn shared two stories that buttress the importance of having the right people in your team.

First is the story of the founders of the popular ice-cream company, CoolHaus. The co-founder of CoolHaus, Freya Estreller and her partner, Natasha Case, believed that a particular angel investor was a great fit for their budding company. This investor had earlier invested in a cookie company that was a co-packer of CoolHaus, so Estreller believed working with the investor would be strategic. But contrary to what they had thought, the partnership did not go as planned. The investor was concerned with the company's day-to-day running and didn't allow any room for mistakes. Such close supervision could be suffocating and unhealthy for a startup. Fortunately for CoolHaus, the investor agreed to convert his equity to debt.

CoolHaus would go on to land $1 million in funding from Bobby Margolis, a former CEO of Cherokee Group. Margolis was a perfect contrast to the first investor. He looked at the bigger picture and was not interested in the daily operations of the company. All he was interested in was to make the company grow into an international brand. Sharing what the experience with the first investor taught her, Estreller said, "We mistook common interests for common vision." She advised businesses to "be clear about the value, beyond money, that your investor adds to your business." In 2014, the company raked in about $6 million in revenue.[7] *Forbes* recorded that in 2018, they had gross revenues of $11 million.[8] This was possible because they corrected their mistake and worked with the right kind of person.

The second story is of Deepti Sharma Kapur, owner of FoodtoEat, an online ordering service where customers get access to restaurants, food trucks, and caterers. Kapur, desperately needing a team to build her customer base, made a big mistake: she hired too quickly, and in the process, hired salespeople who neither understood the company nor its vision.

They were only looking for jobs. At a point, she had to let some of them go. The experience taught her to rely on references from people in her industry. Kapur said that the first question she asks when she wants to recruit is, "What do you know about the industry and our company?" This new approach gave her company a boost. As of 2014 when Donna Fenn shared this story, the company was working with more than 900 food vendors and served corporate clients like Tumblr. In 2013, the company grossed a revenue of $500,000.[9]

Atmosphere

Like a meteorologist, the entrepreneur must be able to study the business atmosphere and use his study to make informed decisions. Meteorologists are not psychics, so they cannot accurately tell what the weather will look like tomorrow, next week, next month, or next year. They only make *educated* guesses, which may be right or wrong. But right, most times. Likewise, you should be able to study your atmosphere and make educated predictions of the future using past and present events. So how do you do this? The answer is simple: research.

Your level of knowledge cannot go beyond the level of information you have. You cannot predict economic or market trends if your knowledge about the economy or market is shallow.

There are three forms of knowledge for making educated guesses or forecasts about the industry or market. They are qualitative knowledge, quantitative knowledge, and knowledge of causal relationships.

Qualitative knowledge

This is subjective knowledge. It is knowledge obtained through market research and interactions with industry experts. Here, you ask the question: *What knowledge can I gain from my studies, interactions, and experiences?* It analyzes present events, although interviewed experts may relate these present events to past ones. *Investopedia* stated that it deals with "intangible, inexact concerns that belong to the social and experiential realm rather than the mathematical one."[10] Here, you would rely on observation, insights, and industry experience. There are several methods of obtaining qualitative knowledge. Smallbusiness.chron.com outlines four of these methods: Delphi Method, Jury of Executive Opinion, Grassroots Forecasting, and Market Research.[11]

- *Delphi Method*: This is a consensus approach where experts gather to air their views and deliberate on *an* event or issue. The convening of experts in such a situation may become an ego contest, a display of hubris spurred by knowledge and, maybe, wealth. An expert with a strong personality may want to overshadow the opinions of others. To solve this problem, the Delphi approach requires that experts fill out questionnaires and surveys independently, instead of meeting face to face. An analysis team reviews the answers, making changes where necessary to the review material. The team repeats this process until a consensus emerges.

- *Jury of Executive Opinion*: Here, you rely on the opinions of high-level managers. For instance, you may gather department managers or advisory board members, present them with company or industry statistical data, request their opinion, and arrive at a consensus.[12]

- *Grassroots Forecasting*: With this method, you obtain knowledge from those closest to the end user. You ask them about consumer perception and consumer expectation. The responses obtained would help you make informed decisions regarding your product or service—and how to make it *fit* for the end user.

- *Market research*: This is a level ahead of grassroots forecasting. Here, you meet with the end users directly. You obtain subjective, qualitative data through consumer survey, interviews, and/or panels, then use these data to make "accurate predictions about the size, scope, demographics, and buying habits"[13] of your market.

There is an important point to note about qualitative knowledge. Same way you, the entrepreneur, tries to gather knowledge about the market, is the same way the market gathers information or knowledge about you and your company. You want to gain knowledge about the market so that you can fashion your products and services to meet the market, but how do you know the market would be willing to patronize you? For this reason, you need to position yourself so that when the market carries out its own research on you, you would be found worthy.

A lot of companies fail to do this and then wonder why they record poor sales even when they have done their homework. Customers also do their homework, and a minor flaw can turn a customer off. Tim Smith pointed out that customers are more crucial to a company's success than the management and employees since customers are the source of revenue.[14]

Customers are the direct recipient of a company's actions, whether good or bad. This is why Smith advised that an investor looking to invest in a company should try being a customer first. In an example, Smith said that if an investor was considering investing in an airline with excellent financial performance, such an investor should try being a customer. Suppose on trying to use the airline, the investor finds a bug-ridden website, cranky customer reps, petty extra fees, and resentful passengers, it becomes obvious that the company does not prioritize its customers.[15]

Qualitative knowledge is subjective and may be tainted by bias. But an entrepreneur who allows his bias or emotions to becloud his business sense and objectivity is not yet mature to lead. Business, most times, is about doing what is best, not what you *feel* is best. Cognitive bias has been shown to be one of the reasons business leaders make poor decisions. Norman Marks, a global thought leader and internal auditor, revealed that he had been affected by cognitive bias while making business decisions. He trusted people because of their charm instead of challenging their knowledge of the subject. He hired individuals with perfect resumes and certifications instead of others who probably were more creative and curious. He respected those in authority to the point that he ignored the fact that they could default on their commitments.[16]

As an entrepreneur, study the market and take decisions according to market conditions.

Quantitative knowledge

This is knowledge obtained through historical market data. Here, you predict the future of the market using past trends. You ask yourself: *What information can I get from market trends and patterns?* You collect and analyze measurable and verifiable data such as revenues and market share in order to understand the activity and performance of a business or industry.[17] With quantitative knowledge, you do not have to rely on your instincts or experience to make business decisions. Everything you need lies in the trends and patterns in the market.

There is one fundamental fact every entrepreneur should know: there is nothing new in the world. Everything we see has happened before. So, when you get into an industry to start a business, it is important you analyze what has happened and position yourself to get a sizable share of the industry.

One mistake many entrepreneurs often make is that they focus so much on their desire to be innovative that they forget that innovation is not only about creating something *entirely* new. Innovation also means improving on what is existing. Ross Simmonds, a digital strategist and marketer, stated that innovation happens from imitation.[18] This is what you should gun for when analyzing market data. Your aim should be to spot trends and patterns, and build your business according to these trends and patterns. Check what has existed before and replicate an improved version.

Instagram copied the Stories feature from Snapchat. Sega took a cue from Nintendo's *Super Mario* to create the game, *Sonic the Hedgehog*. Xiaomi's user interface is remarkably similar to Apple's. These companies have used the imitation game to gain a sizable portion of the market. Although Facebook does not release the revenue numbers of Instagram, it was predicted that in 2016, Instagram had a revenue of about $2 billion, towering far above Snapchat's $463.1 million. With the release of *Sonic the Hedgehog*, Sega took 55 percent of the market, displacing Nintendo which once accounted for 90% of America's video game industry in 1990. Xiaomi may not have ousted Apple from its top position in the smartphone market, but by imitating Apple, the company made a revenue of about $14.5 billion in 2017.[19] These companies were able to record breakthroughs because they worked with past trends and patterns and positioned themselves in the market.

There is a confluence point where quantitative knowledge and qualitative knowledge meet. Qualitative knowledge gathers information from the market, interactions with business players, and entrepreneurial experience. Removing the layers from qualitative knowledge, we would discover that it is a knowledge most times backed by quantitative aspects of the market. Qualitative information or knowledge is simply the surface outlook or the finished form of quantitative information. Kimberlee Leonard puts it better when she stated that quantitative data tells us what is happening, while qualitative data seeks to develop underlying reasons for the data.[20]

A simple case study to understand this confluence is what goes on in the stock or cryptocurrency markets. The candlesticks show the trends and patterns of the market within a certain time frame. This is quantitative data. Technical analysts study these candlesticks and predict what is going on in the market—at what price level is there a concentration of demand, at what price level is there a concentration of supply, what is the market sentiment? An investor who studies these charts would be able to determine the right time and price to enter and exit the market.

For you as an entrepreneur, the data you get from the Delphi method, Jury of Executive Opinion, and so on are birthed not only from experience and instinct, but also from quantitative data. Use this data to position yourself favorably in the market. Do not allow your emotions or sentiments becloud your decisions. Now, this is not to say that there is no place for instinct in business. There is. But following instinct is discretionary. There is no formula to tell how to make use of your instinct. If your instinct has always led you down the right path, then trust it. But also trust the numbers too. Numbers don't lie.

Knowledge of causal relationships

You obtain this knowledge by marrying cause and effect. You predict the outcome of one event based on the functioning of another. The question asked here is: *If that happens, what happens to this?* As an entrepreneur, you should not trivialize certain situations or events, because even the most minor event can impact your business. A macroeconomic variable as basic as the GDP of a nation can affect an entire product database.[21]

There are mathematical and statistical variables used to study causal relationships. This is not a mathematics or statistics text, so I wouldn't bore and bug you with such information. However, I came up with certain variables which you need to watch out for as an entrepreneur. I divided these variables into two groups: external variables and internal variables.

The external variables are factors outside your control which could have a positive or negative impact on your business. There are six variables in this group and are popularly referred to as PESTLE factors or variables. They are politics & policies, economic, social, technological, legal, and environmental factors.

The internal variables are factors within your control; factors within your organization. They are purely human factors: you—the entrepreneur, and your team—employees and investors. We have discussed the internal variables in chapter one and we will also see them in other chapters. For this reason, this chapter will only focus on the external variables.

- **Politics & policies.** An entrepreneur should not neglect politics. This is not to say that you must dabble into politics and governance. But as an entrepreneur, you should know that politics and governance birth policies that can impact your business for the better or the worse. This is why top business moguls anticipate elections of their home countries and even other countries—like the US, UK, Russia, and China—that control the global economy. We have seen cases of governments imposing tax laws or trade tariffs that affect businesses. As a matter of fact, it was the tax laws of certain governments that gave rise to illegal structures like tax havens, and legal ones like tax inversion.

Modern-day innovations like robotics and blockchain technology are focused on building decentralized systems that cannot be regulated by the government. This is because over time, we have witnessed the overregulation by the government stifle the growth and innovation of businesses. Businesses have left certain countries or moved their headquarters to other countries because of stringent laws. In 2014,

Burger King left the United States for Canada. With that move, the company saved about $275 million in taxes.[22]

The politics of your home country and that where your business is domiciled should concern you. For instance, New Zealand has been ranked the *best* place for doing business according to 2018 report by the *Wall Street Journal*.[23] The country still ranked number 1 in 2019 according to the World Bank.[24] It is a country not just with a free economy, but one with a stable democracy. The government encourages businesses to invest and create jobs. The country favors foreign direct investment and encourages entrepreneurs to expand into New Zealand. Manufacturing businesses easily thrive in the country because of its robust infrastructure, good transportation network, logistics services, and energy production. The country allows foreign entrepreneurs to apply for loans and funding. It is also a country fraught with startup accelerators, venture capitalists, and local business investors.[25]

Based on simple causal relationships, we can easily deduce that a business set up in New Zealand has every chance to be successful. Your knowledge of causal relationships between the political atmosphere and the business world in such a country enables you to take sound decisions for your business. This is not to say that a country like New Zealand does not pose a challenge to businesses, especially foreign companies. For example, the Prime Minister of New Zealand, Jacinda Arden had made statements antagonizing immigration and foreign investments. In 2018, the parliament passed a law preventing non-resident foreigners from acquiring property in the country.[26] Say you had a desire to expand in New Zealand even though it is neither your country of origin or residence, such antagonism from its leader and the law passed by the parliament already suggest that expanding into that country may be impossible—at worst, and tough—at best.

This brings me to my next point: study leaders. It is important you study the lives of leaders—study their beliefs, their culture, and their ideologies. By doing this, you would know what to expect when they come into power. There are leaders whose entry into power determines if your business would thrive or die. A leader that understands entrepreneurship would most likely make laws that favor businesses. Indonesia's president, Joko Widodo is a good example.

Widodo, the seventh president of Indonesia has a business background. He is the first president of Indonesia with a business background. Before taking the mantle of leadership, Joko Widodo owned a small furniture business. His vice, Jusuf Kalla was also a business mogul (built the Kalla business empire from his home province) before getting into politics. The Joko-Kalla duo used their business knowledge to cut red tapes which slowed down businesses. The duo also improved the country's World Bank's Ease of Doing Business index from 104th to 73rd position.[27]

Now, there have been debates stating that laws became favorable for businesses in Widodo's tenure not because the government wanted to favor business owners, but because principal actors in government own businesses.[28] While this may be the case, it does not rule out the causal relationship between Widodo's leadership and Indonesia's entrepreneurial climate. A foresighted entrepreneur who has studied the life of Widodo would have positioned their company to benefit from the new policies.

Have foresight. Be knowledgeable. Predict likely events that may occur with a change in power or policy, then position yourself to benefit from it—if it would be a positive change, or avoid it—if it would be negative.

- **Economic Factors.** As an entrepreneur, you may choose not to bother about how national and international politics impact your business, but you *must* be concerned about the economy. The economy revolves around wealth, money. And what sustains your business is money. So if the economy is affected, your business would also be affected. It is the most direct causal relationship of all the factors. A small shift in the economic balance could cause a large change in your business.

49

BBC UK noted that the economic climate can impact a business in four major ways: unemployment, changing levels of consumer income, interest rates, and tax rates.[29] So how do these sub-variables affect your business?

For BBC UK, unemployment is not just a state where people are out of jobs; it is a situation where the economy is not fully utilizing the workers available.[30] When this happens, households have less income and reduced purchasing power. And this has a direct impact on businesses. There would be lower sales and, consequently, lower revenue. Lower revenue means that the company may be unable to pay salaries. Inability to pay salaries would lead to laying off workers. And the cycle continues.

However, unemployment may become beneficial to certain businesses. As a result of poor purchasing power, consumers seek cheaper alternatives, which are often less-quality goods and services. The owners of these alternatives experience a boost in sales, thus directly benefiting from unemployment.[31] As an entrepreneur, you can decide which result of unemployment you would want to ride on. Would unemployment affect your business negatively, or is there a way to use it to your advantage? Amazon did the latter, as we would see later in this chapter.

Unemployment can also impact the level of consumer income. It is expected that in a country where unemployment is at its peak, citizens would have lower income and reduced purchasing power. But in a case where the economy thrives and citizens enjoy a high, steady income, then there is a propensity for higher spending.

There is this thing that money does to a person. When you are broke, you live by a scale of preference. You know that you cannot meet all your needs at the same time. So, when you are at the grocery store or a clothing store, you go for only what is necessary and affordable. But this changes as soon as money comes. Maybe you won a lottery or got a raise—your purchasing will and power become heightened. There is a propensity for you to even spend on what you do not need.

Now, the wise entrepreneur can take advantage of this trend. When there is economic prosperity, your thoughts as an entrepreneur should be channeled into making products or services that attract customers. The truth is many have money, but they do not know where or how to spend their money. The onus lies on you to be creative with your products and services. Give people what they need in a way they've never seen before—and their money becomes yours.

Variables like interest rates and taxes are also important. They impact the overall cost of your business. This is why news about behemoth companies avoiding taxes never gets old. The discourse on corporate tax is a complex one. It is not just a financial discourse, but a moral one.

On the one hand, companies *should* pay taxes to countries where they have a presence. These taxes are for the benefit of the citizens. But on the other hand, there is a situation where the governments of these countries do not use these taxes for the socioeconomic development of the country and its people. Companies know this, so they avoid paying. It becomes a story of the fight between two elephants and the grasses being collateral damage.

During the Covid-19 pandemic, giant tech companies like Facebook, Google, and Microsoft avoided tax in developing nations to the tune of almost $3 billion. ActionAid, an international NGO committed to working against poverty and injustice, pointed out that that sum "could pay for 729,010 nurses, 770,649 midwives or 879,899 primary school teachers annually in 20 countries across Africa, Asia and South America."[32]

While interest rates and taxes directly impact the cost of your business, you have to strike a balance between taking the financially smart option or the morally unethical option. I understand that when it comes to these issues, there are a lot of grey areas. To do the right thing, there should be interplay of your business sense and moral codes.

- **Social Factors.** The social climate of a place shapes the behavior of the people and what they buy. Social variables are vast. They range from lifestyle and education to religion and social classes. This is another aspect of your PESTLE analysis where you need to strike a balance. You are an entrepreneur. You are human—a social being, not a robot.

You have your beliefs, values, sexuality, principles, religion, habits, and every other quality that makes you human. And your business is serving different people with diverse social characteristics. Thus, you are bound to experience social conflicts in your entrepreneurial journey. It will be unwise to allow these conflicts interfere with your business. This is a mistake you should *never* make.

Your brand, products, and services should not discriminate or stereotype individuals or communities no matter your religious, sexual, ethnic, or racial inclinations. Drop your inclinations at the door and embrace humanity. Some popular companies did this after the death of George Floyd and the subsequent outrage that followed. PepsiCo scrapped its 130-year-old breakfast brand, Aunt Jemima after admitting that the image of the black woman originated from a racial stereotype. Colgate stated that it would rebrand its top-selling Chinese toothpaste, Darlie whose original name was Darkie, meaning "black person toothpaste." Dixie Beer asked the public to help them pick a new name because it wanted to change its name which has connotations of slavery.[33]

Being a socially aware brand can do a lot of good to your business. As humans, we are social beings. This is why social topics are sensitive issues. They affect our emotions and sense of value. People do not want to be associated with brands that do not consider their emotional wellbeing and sense of value. In recent years, we have seen our societies morph into places with high energy and a strong desire for freedom. We are no longer in a world where people cower in silence to the dictates of superior individuals or corporate bodies. People speak out. Social media has made the average person a media house, a loud voice. And speaking out plus the cancel culture we now see, can leave a *permanent* dent to your brand and company.

Many entrepreneurs and business managers neglect the impact social issues can have on their business. Recall, we are talking about causal relationships. As an entrepreneur, you have to understand the social climate of the world. In this current world, anything you say or do may be used against you in the court of social media. There is a mob online waiting to lynch you without giving you a fair trial. Michael Hogan wrote that there is "a barrage of judgement waiting to be unleashed at the smallest provocation." He went further to state that "every nook and cranny of an organization is subject to scrutiny. What used to be relatively simple is now anything but, and organizations are left damned if they do and if they don't."[34] This may be complicated and exhausting, but it is important you bear it in mind so as to take actions that wouldn't put your business at risk.

Social issues are too weighty to ignore that the outrage can even start from your employees. Jack Kelly, a senior contributor for *Forbes*, pointed out that in the past, employees followed company orders without question. But that has changed. He wrote that there is a wave of employees given to activism who intentionally seek employment in companies who share their social and ethical beliefs. If they happen to be in a company that derails from any of their core beliefs, these employees protest immediately.[35] This was the case with online home goods and furniture company, Wayfair.

In 2019, the company had sold bedroom furniture worth about $200,000 to a government contractor who operated immigration detention centers on the US-Mexico border. Hundreds of Wayfair employees were displeased with this—they didn't want their company to profit off children being in concentration camps. They expressed their displeasure to management, asking for the sales to be canceled. When the CEO refused to comply with the demands, the workers staged a walkout.[36]

It was a complicated case, which started a two-sided debate. Those on the side of management argued that if those beds weren't sold, then the children in those camps would have slept on cold, hard floors. But pro-employees countered this argument by stating that if the company were interested in the children, they would have donated the beds instead of profiting from it.[37] The company ended up donating the profit made from the sales to the Red Cross.[38]

The story of Wayfair underscores how significant the effects of social conflicts could be to a company. Jack Kelly went ahead to paint a picture of other negative results that could have played out depending on how the public reacted to the protest. Kelly stated that the protests could have backfired on the employees (and the company) in several ways. One: Amazon is one of Wayfair's biggest competitors. If consumers had decided to support employees and trigger the cancel culture, they would have boycotted Wayfair's products. This would have meant lesser sales and revenue. The company would have had to lay off employees to cut cost. Two: If a staff who had protested was fired, the staff might perceive it as a penalty for participating in the protests. Such staff may go ahead to sue the company. Three: Staff who are not promoted or given salary raises or bonuses may also perceive that they are being punished for taking part in the protests, especially if staff who didn't participate in the protests get promoted or a salary raise or bonus. These three scenarios could culminate into a toxic work environment.[39]

- **Technological factors.** Business demands a lot of you—production, distribution, marketing, sales, etc. Thus, it is only wise that you adopt up-to-date techniques for running your business. Irrespective of what your business entails, it is necessary to use technologies to facilitate business processes.

Although we are moving towards an era of utmost dependence on machines, technology does not downplay the importance of human resources—they only help improve business operations and guarantee absolute productivity.

The development of technology has played a significant role in business development, especially in automating processes. Automated processes *directly* influence and increase productivity and reach. Kweilin Ellingrud pointed out that automation can handle 45 percent of repetitive tasks—and give workers time for higher-value tasks like problem-solving and creating new ideas.[40] In the end, there is smooth production and distribution of goods and services, healthy customer relationships, and a flexible working environment.

Furthermore, technology helps maintain healthy business relationships. Internet technology like Skype helps you to connect with your workers. And social media platforms like Facebook, Instagram, and Twitter enable you to access your customers directly without the need for a physical meeting. This means that at any time, you can maintain human connections—a vital ingredient for any business to thrive.

In chapter one, we saw an exposition on fads and disruptions. In this era, every fad or disruption will come as new technology. So, have foresight. Be knowledgeable enough to spot disruptions when they appear. Remember, companies that took advantage of the internet in its early days are big winners today. I know you would want to remind me of the internet bubble of the 2000s. But know this: markets crash from time to time, but a market or industry with resilience is one you should be in. More than two decades after the crash, the internet is here.

- **Legal factors.** Every business is subject to the law of the land in which it operates. The corporate laws of the nation where your business operates govern, to a large extent, the mode of operations of your business. Legal factors are closely related to the first variable in the PESTLE analysis: politics. And we have seen how politics and policies can positively or negatively affect a business. However, we will turn our focus on how legal factors can affect your business independent of politics.

Legal experts, Samuel D. Brickley and Brian M. Gottesman, stated that the essence of laws is to create standards, resolve disputes, maintain order and protect the rights of citizens.[41]

As a business owner, you would not be comfortable with every law. However, you must be aware of these laws and their relationship with your business.

Legal factors that could impact your business include laws on taxation, organizational law, consumer laws, employment regulations, securities and immigration, contract laws, intellectual properties law, etc. Let's see some of them.

Organizational Law

This is probably the fundamental legal factor that has a significant stronghold on businesses. From a business name to the type of entity selected before registration, this law determines the scope of activities of a business. Organizational law also manages the creation, operation, and termination of a business. The legal status of a company (e.g., limited liability company or a limited liability partnership) determines its taxation, employee, and customs regulations.

Employment Law

Chapter one looked at selecting your team. Besides being guided by personal principles, there is also a legal side to choosing your team, your employees especially. Employment law focuses on the welfare of employees, including mode of payment, work ethics, etc. This law gives employees the right to report any form of misconduct exhibited by their employers to the authorities. In other words, it ensures that the employer and employees maintain a healthy relationship without any form of discrimination based on gender, color, religion, or race. When you align this with the social variables and the real-life cases we saw earlier, you would understand why employees can take drastic decisions such as a protest against management.

Consumer law

Consumer laws are designed to facilitate legal relationships between consumers and business owners, and protect consumers from fraudulent companies. You may wonder how this affects your business if it's all about the customer. It affects you because these laws ensure that you do not make the customer uncomfortable during patronage and after patronage as they use your product. For example, business owners are expected to disclose a reasonable amount of information about their policies, products, and services to the public. So irrespective of what you do, your customers have the right to know basic details about your products.

Intellectual properties law

This law is designed to protect products or services such as books, machines, music, or paintings created via a human mind, ensuring that no one takes credit for them without the owner's permission. It gives a person or business the right to sole ownership. However, someone else can use the property if the owner permits. And the rights of such a person are also protected under the law. Chapter five will show how some top companies used this law as their "indirect army" to stay on top of their industry.

Products and services law

The products and services you provide as a businessperson must be checked and tested to ensure that they are suitable for consumption by the target market. The standard of a product or service is checked based on the ingredients used, manufacturing process, environment, the professional status of producers, and quality. However, product laws vary depending on business location.

Taxation

Just like organizational law, the growth of a business depends on the tax regulations in a state. Some states/countries are more tax-friendly than others. That is why businesses in some states flourish more than others in other states. Business owners are strongly advised to first observe and understand the tax policies in a given state before rolling out products and services. As stated earlier, taxation is an important factor that it has led to practices like tax evasion and tax inversion.

Antitrust law

This law is particularly for businesses with a similar target audience or similar market structure. Due to unhealthy competitions and rivalries that could spring up between two or more businesses, this law ensures equal and healthy competitions by regulating business activities, such as price-fixing, bid-rigging, and unfair monopoly. But if competitors understand that they could collaborate, maybe this law would not have existed.

Other examples of legal factors that affect businesses include health and safety law, import and export law, and fraud law.

While these laws appear cumbersome, they determine the growth of any business in a geographical area and are mostly not negotiable.

- **Environmental Factors.** They determine the nature of a product or service and consumers' reactions to them. For example, no one will readily purchase a heater in an already hot environment. This means that if you must record reasonable growth in business, your product—depending on your industry—must align with the weather conditions of your business environment.

Although no business, small and large, has control over these factors, marketing strategies could be developed around these environmental factors to have an accurate picture of market trends and how your business can thrive in a particular area.

There are various environmental factors affecting business development, such as climate change, green agenda, environmental policies, pollution, natural resources, pandemics, recycling, waste disposal, etc.

Environmental policy

The major environmental factor affecting businesses is environmental policy. Environmental policy is the commitment of a business to government regulations and other policy mechanisms that revolve around environmental issues. No business progresses without adhering to environmental policies, as the law compels organizations to change their operational routine to meet stipulated standards.

These environment policies also vary depending on the type of business and the natural features peculiar to that environment. For example, the environmental policies for a company that deals with the production of food items are different from the policies guiding a skincare company. But these policies ensure there is a conducive environment for all to grow simultaneously.

Climate change

Another environmental factor that determines the success of a business is climate change. Climate change can be a threat to businesses if not taken into proper consideration. With the increasing issue of global warming and hostile weather conditions in recent years, it is difficult for organizations to operate equally in every weather condition. Agricultural-based businesses that directly depend on an adequate water supply to grow will be affected if climatic changes result in reduced rainfalls. Although erecting an irrigation system could be an option in such cases, it is expensive and might only be plausible for large-scale businesses.

As a business owner, you must have first-hand knowledge of your business, understand that it is susceptible to climatic changes, and identify favorable areas. Are your products and services suitable for all weather types? Interestingly, consumers are also becoming aware of this factor and are most likely to patronize brands that align with their environment, as they seek both satisfaction and convenience.

Green Agenda

Business-related activities affect the environment as much as the environment affects the growth of businesses. Every business owner must understand the need to have environmental-friendly policies to achieve desired business goals. The Green Agenda is an example of a friendly environmental policy that helps organizations manage their operations to ensure minimal impact on the local and global environment.

To be environmentally accountable, you need to develop operational plans which are beneficial to both the company and the physical environment. These plans must highlight the mode of production and operation, waste management system, and general work ethics.

Pollution

Environmental pollution is not a new phenomenon, but it is one of the greatest problems facing humanity.

Both developed and underdeveloped regions have a fair share of this burden. Pollution is also one of the primary environmental factors that affect business strategies. It can cause some major environmental events, resulting in the disruption of supply chains or a relative increase in the cost of raw materials for production.

Business owners need to monitor such events and develop subsequent plans to tackle them. Your ability to stay in business during any event that threatens your physical environment depends on how well you plan.

Environmental pollution includes air pollution, water pollution, soil pollution, etc. Air pollution is most peculiar to organizations that constantly emit pollutants, which are detrimental to human health and the planet in general. If your business poses a threat to the planet, then you should reevaluate your policies. You should also consider the potential health effects of a polluted environment on your employees, as poor air quality is a risk to employees' health, overall well-being, and ability to perform their duties judiciously.

Contaminated air can also affect your workers indoors as well as outdoors. So do not ignore indoor pollutants, as they can eventually lead to the loss of employees. And when this happens, you will be made to face the consequences of your action, which may lead to the collapse of your business. Make a conscious effort to guarantee the safety of your staff by ensuring they have quality air void of indoor toxins. No one wants to work for a business that cares less about the health of its workers.

A threat to your business is a threat to the economy and vice versa. This clearly explains the collective impact of employee health. Poor air quality can also affect the reach and growth of your business. Regions with above-average levels of air pollution are often seen as undesirable cities to live or work in. So the chances of you attracting skilled employees and direct consumers are relatively low. Even with enough serenity within the company to retain, train and promote current employees, business growth could still be hindered.

A survey conducted by Bain and Company, and the American Chamber of Commerce in China, disclosed that 52% of American-owned businesses operating in China experienced difficulty in gaining senior-skill-level employees. And one of the biggest contributors to this shortage was the level of air pollution in the area.[42]

The negative impact of air pollution on business performance seems overwhelming. But an increase in public awareness can guarantee improved performance beyond the current state of things. You should invest in the working conditions of your staff, uphold good company morals, create growth opportunities, and improve your company's overall environmental position. Public awareness will also help you boost your company's image and credibility.

Note that modern technological advancements allow companies, individuals, and the government to detect the effect of pollution on health and the economy. And sooner than later, this detection will enable the tracing of these effects back to the source, revealing companies that are actively constituting havoc to the environment. You do not want your business or organization to be found guilty.

Natural resources

Availability of natural resources is an important environmental factor as most businesses have natural resources as their major raw material. Little or no natural resources can hinder the production and productivity of a company. While seeking to grow your business, identify places that have your required raw materials for production.

It is important to note that sometimes, your consumers' location may differ from where your raw materials are located. So, you need to strike a balance—devise plans on how you can reach your raw materials and still be accessible to your direct consumers. These plans may or may not be cost-effective. But the value of your business will determine how much you are willing to spend to get desired results.

For example, if your target audience is in Nigeria and raw materials required for production are in South Africa, you could seek for partnership with companies that supply those necessary materials. You can also find other ways to produce these raw materials for continued production.

Pandemics

Even before the outbreak of the coronavirus pandemic, the World Economic Forum has constantly warned about the adverse effects of pandemics on businesses through its publication, *Outbreak Readiness and Business Impact*.[43]   It was like a premonition, a prophecy, which came to pass in 2020 with the Covid-19 pandemic which affected both the local and global economy.   The pandemic also resulted in high mortality and caused many businesses to shut down.   Many organizations that lacked a social media presence struggled to keep in touch with their customers.   Others that could not integrate the internet into their business recorded poor sales.

From the Covid-19 outbreak, we could see that pandemics do not only affect health, but threaten the economies of nations, disrupt business operations, and limit day-to-day activities.   Therefore, the world is adjusting one step at a time.   Businesses are attaining sustainable models and diversifying their public approach.   You should do it too. You should equip yourself by building a strong virtual connection with your employees. Ensure that they uphold basic work-from-home ethics when necessary, procure substantial health insurance for all, and organize virtual classes to equip them for the virtual era.   Your workforce could also be made of remote and physical workers, especially if your business is not limited to a physical location.

You should also invest in digital marketing, social media marketing, and other remote methods to help you sustain the relationship with your customers.   To be on the safer side, build your business framework to be formidable so it can outlive anything worse than the Covid-19 pandemic. In other words, endeavor to set long-term business goals.

Recycling

Recycling is one of the major environmental factors that supports a greener business environment.

How does your business account for waste disposal? How often do you recycle waste materials?   Instead of littering the environment with waste materials such as paper, glass, and plastic, do you recycle them for further production? Recycling waste materials provides alternatives to preserve virgin resources and keep the environment safe. It also saves you the stress and cost of purchasing raw materials.

Although there has been a positive trend towards recycling waste materials, many businesses still dump wastes in landfills. This affects consumers and workers and increases the cost of cleaning the environment in which the business operates. To create a balance, you should consider producing less waste, recycle them, and use them for further productions.

The attack is as important as the drawing board. It is like a footballer putting all he has practiced to work in a real game. Never leave any stone unturned. Get the right knowledge. Forecast. Attack. Win.

Pledge to Action

I affirm that:

I am not afraid to attack.

I will launch every plan I have drafted on the drawing board.

I will leave no stone unturned.

I will use every qualitative knowledge, quantitative knowledge, and knowledge of causal relationships to my benefit.

I will not be caught unawares by any external variables.

I cannot wait to win.

So I will attack right away.

CHAPTER THREE

The Strategy

"Strategy is about setting yourself apart from the competition. It's not a matter of being better at what you do – it's a matter of being different at what you do."

— Michael Porter

Y our strategy as an entrepreneur does not begin when you get to the battlefield; it begins the moment you conceive your vision. Many entrepreneurs make a mistake when developing a strategy —they seek to be better than the competition. This is not wrong *per se*, but it is limiting. When you aim to be better, all you are trying to do is improve on an already existing idea. And there is a possibility that your own improvement can also be improved upon. So do not aim to be better; aim to be distinct. This should be your primary strategy. One company that aims for distinction, is Apple.

In an exposition on Apple's generic and intensive growth strategies, Pauline Meyer noted that the generic strategy of the company is broad differentiation. It is a strategy that focuses on key features that distinguish the company and its IT products from competitors. Some of these key features include elegant design and user-friendliness of products, combined with high-end branding.[1]

Apple's sense of innovation and distinction made them the big leaders they are today in the smartphone market. When other phone companies like Blackberry were only focused on improving the software of their products, Apple became the first company to produce all-screen phones that were devoid of physical keyboards. Today we can hardly recall what a phone with a physical keyboard looks like.

Elon Musk didn't aim to be better by improving on gasoline cars; he strove for distinction. And that birthed Tesla cars. Tesla vehicles revolutionized the world of electric cars. Before their advent, electric vehicles had no market appeal. They were unsatisfactory, ugly, heavy, and took a long time to charge. But Tesla came with "the design of a sports car, the safety of a Toyota, and could charge in minutes rather than the hours it took earlier EVs to get juiced up."[2] For Musk, he didn't just create cars, he created "laptops on wheels."[3]

It is not enough to distinguish yourself from the crowd, you have to also maintain this distinction. Being different can come with its own challenges. For instance, your product may not be mainstream as you would like. But you need not worry as long as you know you are offering value no one else offers. iPhones are not as mainstream as Android devices.

Apple controls just about 13 percent of the smartphone market globally[4], yet the company rakes in billions of dollars yearly. *Statista* reported that in the fourth quarter of 2020, the company generated $26.44 billion in revenue from the sale of iPhones.[5] Apple's strategy and company culture tells us that all we need is to provide top value to the world, and we would attract the right kind of customers who appreciate this value and are ready to pay for it.

When it comes to strategy, there are five key points you and your team need to know in order to sustain your victory. These key points, as outlined by Vu, are:

1. **Know when to and when not to fight.** As an entrepreneur, there would be times you would feel like going with the buzz in the industry. It may seem as though the competition is getting ahead. But do not panic. Do not rush in making decisions. Study the market and choose your battles wisely. If you panic,

you may likely fall into the trap of doing what others are doing, and when this happens, you lose your uniqueness. You become just like every other business.

Before iPhones hit the market, Blackberry dominated. But Apple didn't just jump into creating a product to rival Blackberry. Blackberry stayed in the global market for over ten years and gained so much popularity. Now, the question is: Where was iPhone all the while? I want to think that Steve Jobs and the rest of the Apple team were busy observing and studying the market within that period. They probably investigated Blackberry's flaws by asking its users what they would want in a phone. They thought about the best innovation that would outpace and outclass Blackberry and other phones. Apple spent over ten years allowing Blackberry to rule the market. The company never launched an attack for over ten years. They chose when to fight, to attack. And when they did, it was a flawless victory abetted by Blackberry's lackadaisical approach towards innovation.

2. **Know how to use more troops.** As your vision and company expand, you would need more hands in your team. Never be afraid to try new hands (but that will be after you have taught them the company's vision, values, and culture.) Also, using more troops doesn't only mean utilizing human resources, it also means using new technologies. In this technological age, always try to be among the first to adopt new technology in your business or industry. Think outside the box. In fact, think as if there's no box . Study emerging technologies such as artificial intelligence, 5G, Internet of Things, serverless computing, biometrics, augmented reality/virtual reality, blockchain, robotics, natural language processing, and quantum computing to see how they could be relevant in your business. Be a pioneer. Let technology be part of your troops.

3. **Have the same goal and spirit in all ranks.** Once your team is in line with your vision, they would maintain the company's goal and spirit. I would want to believe that no team member

from Apple felt like jumping ship when Blackberry was ruling the smartphone market. I would want to believe that every member of the Apple team knew that their goal was to be different, thus they weren't moved by their competitor's success. They knew that the success of their competitor didn't mean they were failing. I would want to believe that the goal and spirit of Steve Jobs were inherent in the team. They understood seasons and utilized every season to their advantage.

Many company owners are anxious about handing over because they know that some team members have ideologies and goals different from what the company was built on. But this should not be the case. When building a business, think perpetuity. Let your business outlive you. It is over nine years that Steve Jobs passed on, yet Apple has remained strong. The world has never had the cause to say that Jobs' death affected the company's performance. Some CEOs even cede control to another person while alive. Such CEOs understand that this new head of the company would maintain the goal and spirit they had set and built.

4. **A prepared army will always achieve victory over an unprepared army.** Be the prepared one. Be the one whose company positions itself to take advantage of trends and seasons. Be the one whose company aligns itself with emerging technologies. While your competitors are relaxed, prepare yourself. Watch. Study. Plan. Strategize.

5. **A talented general who is not restrained by the king would be victorious in battle.** Never allow anyone to stifle your creativity. Now, this does not mean you wouldn't ask for counsel, however, be smart enough to know which counsel would stifle your creative process and which would prune you to produce better fruits. Just as you shouldn't be restrained, do not also restrain your team. Allow them the freedom of expression, albeit within the confines of the company's vision.

Allow room for mistakes and be prepared to correct them as often as possible. You will harness the maximum potentials inherent in your team if you give them the freedom to express themselves. No one wants to be caged, not even animals. This is why the moment they see an opening, they escape from their cages. We were not built to be caged—freedom of expression births groundbreaking ideas.

You can have all the human, financial, and material resources, but without a strategy—the right strategy—your vision would not go far. The best way to build the perfect strategy is by studying three things: (1) yourself and your company, (2) the market, and (3) your competitors. Little wonder, Sun Vu made the profound statement: "If we know the enemy and know ourselves, then we will not be endangered in a hundred battle engagements. If we know ourselves but not the enemy then for every victory gained we will also suffer a defeat. If we know neither the enemy nor ourselves, then we will never win."

Pledge to Action

I affirm that:

I am not afraid of launching out because I have the right strategy for winning.

I will not just be the best at what I do; I will be different. I will be distinct.

I am innovative.

I know when to fight.

I choose my battles carefully.

I am prepared to use more troops—humans and machines.

I have the capacity to attract the best team.

A team that understands the goal and spirit of the company.

A team that can sustain this goal and spirit, and even transfer it to others.

I have a prepared team, a prepared army—an army marching to victory.

I am talented.

I am a wise general, a smart entrepreneur.

I have the right strategy.

CHAPTER FOUR

The Mystery

"The mysterious is always attractive. People will always follow a vail."

— Bede Jarrett

B y being different, you weaken your competition subtly. You make them struggle to keep up. This was Sun Vu's military disposition. He got victory by making the opposition miserable. He wrote, "We will entrench because we know we are in a position where victory is uncertain; and we attack because we have more than enough resources to win." With such a strategy, it would be difficult for the enemy to predict their moves. And nothing frustrates the soul like uncertainty.

Be a mystery, an enigma. Let your competition be unable to predict your next move. *Entrench* and *observe*. As you do this, always be prepared for victory. Vu put it this way: "The victory of great fighters is not famed for wisdom, nor is it known for bravery. Being prepared for every winning situation is what guarantees a certain victory." Vu went further to list four things a general must do in the place of preparation for victory to be guaranteed. They are range, measure, calculate and weigh.

- **Range.** Here, the general determines the terrain of both sides. As an entrepreneur, this means determining not just your terrain but that of your competitors. From the types of terrain we looked at in chapter one, you'd face stiff competition in the forest and most likely in the canyon. There is little or no competition in the desert, for no one wants to be in the desert. So observe your competition and know what they are doing to navigate the terrain. If it is in the forest, determine if they are among the tall trees or the short shrubs. If it is in the canyon, are they in the gorge, or are they atop the hill? Determine their range—and determine yours too.

- **Measurement.** After determining the range, the general measures both sides to determine how much resources to use. For instance, if you are in the forest and your competition is a tall tree, while you are a short shrub, then you would need more financial and human resources to elevate yourself and make yourself visible. You would need to be innovative, and resources are needed for innovation.

- **Calculation.** Sun Vu stated that the general has to calculate the number of troops on both sides. As an entrepreneur, do not only calculate the number of troops, also determine the quality of troops. Many entrepreneurs are moved by numbers. They see a company with many staff and they automatically feel afraid, yet those staff may be a bunch of figureheads.

I once observed two community pharmacies in my locality. One had just half the number of staff the other pharmacy had, yet their revenue was high. They restocked their shelves almost every week. The other with many staff barely had patients coming in. They had frequent stockouts. I would pass by the pharmacy and see boredom etched on the faces of the staff.

So it is not all about having a large number of people in your team. Employ people according to what you need in your company per time. Have efficiency and effectiveness in mind when creating a team. It may sound harsh, but if there is one thing the Covid-19 pandemic taught companies around the world is that they've been recruiting more hands than they need. For companies to lay off staff in their numbers showed that the pandemic was a drastic event that revealed where many companies were getting it wrong. Suddenly, these companies realized they could do away with some staff to cut costs. Could it be that if these companies had initially employed their staff based on need and efficiency, there would not have been the need to make employees redundant? Amazon never laid off any staff during the pandemic. As a matter of fact, they went on a hiring spree—employing 36,400 people as at the end of June 2020.[1] In 2020 alone, the company created 400,000 jobs, pushing its total number of employees worldwide to 1 million.[2] In your calculation, place quality over quantity. It is better to have ten excellent hands than a hundred mediocre hands.

- **Weigh.** After determining your terrain, resources, and troops, the next step is to weigh your company's strategy, strengths, and weaknesses and those of the competition. Simply put, at the point of weighing is where you carry out and implement your SWOT analysis. What are your strengths? What are your weaknesses? What opportunities do you have? What threats do you face? This analysis gives you a clue about the status of the competition because your area of strength may be your competition's weakness, while your opportunities may likely be their threats.

What will put you ahead of your competition is to be a mystery. Make people wonder how you do it. Always be prepared. Always be a step ahead.

Determine the range of your terrain. Measure your resources. Calculate and evaluate the number and quality of the troops. Weigh your strengths, weaknesses, opportunities, and threats and use them effectively.

Pledge to Action

I affirm that:

I will be an enigma in my industry.

I will always dare to be different.

I will be a step ahead at all times.

I understand that my baby steps are valid.

I know that my steps will give me wings to fly.

I will study the range of my terrain and measure my resources.

I will determine the number and quality of my troops at all times.

I will weigh my strengths and weaknesses and opportunities and threats.

I am ready to employ my observations to get victory.

I know I will win.

Because I am a mystery.

CHAPTER FIVE

The Winning Team

"None of us is as smart as all of us."

— Ken Blanchard

"If everyone is moving forward together, then success takes care of itself."

— Henry Ford

Throughout this book, I have emphasized the importance of building the right team. The statements of Ken Blanchard and Henry Ford highlights the fact that there is a limit to one's success if the *right* team is not behind a vision. The striking quality about teamwork is that its effectiveness is seen no matter where it is employed—whether for a good or negative cause. For instance, Unit 731 was a group of 3,000 researchers in the Imperial Japanese Army who carried out deadly experiments in northeast China between 1937 and 1945. Led by Lieutenant-General Ishii Shiro, the team vivisected prisoners without anesthesia; injected diseases such as syphilis, anthrax, and gonorrhea into subjects; raped female subjects to carry out tests on their fetuses; used prisoners as targets for grenades; burned people alive; and dropped plague-carrying fleas in Chinese villages to study how fast the disease spread. 3,000 to 250,000 people died in a single camp as a result of these experiments.[1] Such horrendous crime carried out by 3,000 persons could only have been possible through teamwork. If there was division in the camp, then maybe some team members would have attempted (and probably succeeded) in saving a large number of the human lab rats. Maybe some team members would have revealed this to relevant authorities so that appropriate action could be taken. But teamwork never let any of these happen. In one accord, 3,000 persons committed crimes against humanity and were never punished for it.[2] That shows us how powerful teamwork is.

Sun Vu classified an army into two types: the direct army and the indirect army. The direct army is what we have talked about so far in this book—human resources. But the effort of the direct army can be greatly amplified by the indirect army. Sun Vu advised generals to take advantage of natural elements like heaven and earth, rivers and oceans in a battle. Natural elements are the indirect army. And according to Vu, it is important to use them for two reasons: (1) "In combat, direct attack on the enemy is very obvious; but what brings about victory is the indirect attack on the side." (2) "A general who understands the use of indirect army has an infinite source of tactics [resources] like heaven and earth, like rivers and oceans, which will never run out."

So, what is the indirect army of the entrepreneur?

The entrepreneur's indirect army is classed into two groups: technology/innovation and climate.

Technology/innovation as an indirect army

Your competition would definitely know your direct army, but it would take a great deal of effort to discover your indirect army. Humans are tangible, social beings. They interact, and through their interactions, your competition would know they are part of your team. But when it comes to technology or innovation, especially software, there is a lesser tendency for your competition to know the technology you employ if you do not make it known. This is where trade secrets come in. Even if they get to know the technology behind your products, they would have to circumvent patent laws to replicate it. Technology/innovation has kept companies like Google, KFC, Coca-Cola, and New York Times ahead of their peers.

Google's search algorithm has been a top secret all these years. The algorithm is ever-evolving, but Google only reveals some of its changes.[3] This has kept the company ahead of other search engines like Bing and Yandex. According to Chuck Price, because of the algorithm, Google has transcended being just another search engine. It has become ubiquitous, a transitive verb, and a dominant online advertising platform that has amassed 87 percent of the global market share.[4]

Kentucky Fried Chicken (KFC) has a secret ingredient that was only known to Colonel Sanders. But before his death, he wrote down the recipe. The original handwritten copy is tucked away in a safe in Kentucky, and only a few employees—who are bound by a confidentiality agreement—know the recipe.[5]

Similarly, Coca-Cola has a secret ingredient. This confidential information is so important to the soda brand that it branded the ingredient a trade secret instead of patenting it since getting a patent would mean disclosing the ingredient.[6]

Trade secrets aren't only peculiar to consumables and information technology, it also applies to areas like books. The New York Times, which has the most influential book list, has not divulged its definition of what makes a book a bestseller. A book that has sold fewer copies can make its list, while a book that has sold more wouldn't make the list. The newspaper, which has won 130 Pulitzer prizes, has refused to share this secret because it fears that publishers would use the information to manipulate sales data to their advantage.[7]

These companies prove the importance of using technology/trade secrets as an army. These four companies listed above are the best in their respective industries because they've learned to use indirect armies their competitors can never know about. They go to prove Sun Vu's words: *In combat, direct attack on the enemy is very obvious; but what brings about victory is the indirect attack on the side.* Everyone knows Colonel Sanders was the brain behind KFC. KFC's competitors know that even though he is long gone, he is still putting them on their toes. That is the definition of direct attack. It is obvious and can be easily defended. Let's imagine that he never disclosed the secret ingredient before his death, KFC would have lost its place in the market. But a trade secret, an indirect attack, keeps putting KFC above the competition all these years.

Your competition understands the importance of your indirect army and wants to do everything they can to know about it. Thus, you have to protect your indirect army at all costs. This is why you shouldn't neglect your direct army. Your direct army can make your indirect army obvious to your competition. This almost happened to Coca-Cola. In 2006, a Coca-Cola employee alongside two accomplices stole the company's secret formula and tried to sell it to its biggest competitor, Pepsi. Being a reputable brand, the rival company alerted Coca-Cola's officials, and the culprits were arrested.[8]

So, I say again: think outside the box. Think up a technology that would distinguish you. This technology or innovation could either be applied to your input or process. It is difficult to employ trade secrets at the output level because at that level, the product or service is ready for distribution to the user. KFC's innovation is at the input—the blending of ingredients. Same as Coca-Cola, New York Times and Google have their innovation at their process—the method of selecting a best-seller, the method of optimizing search results.

Climate as an indirect army

In military warfare, Sun Vu recommended that an army use the elements of nature to their advantage. While you may not use the natural elements to your favor in business, you can use the sociopolitical or economic climate.

- **The sociopolitical climate.** Be smart and sensitive enough to use social issues to your advantage. Discourses on social issues like racism, feminism, domestic violence, and sexuality have gained so much momentum in recent times than before. A smart company would position itself around these issues to market itself. This is a strategy that *must* be applied subtly—because it would come across as insensitive to capitalize on such sensitive issues for the sole purpose of making financial gains. People are smart enough to know when a company is taking advantage of a situation for the sake of making a profit. Once people feel this way about your business, this strategy would backfire. So, show *genuine* concern towards these issues. True, boosting your exposure and profit should be part of your objective, but they should be secondary. Observe the issues that align with your company values and culture, and then offer value to society.

Paul A. Argenti in an article for Harvard Business Review[9], outlined three questions that a company must ask before lending its voice to a social issue.

- *Does the issue align with your company's strategy?*

Argenti backs up what I said earlier. Your strategy is part of your mission and vision, thus the issue should align with what you already believe in and do.

- *Can you meaningfully influence the issue?*

According to Argenti, you need to have the expertise and resources to make a difference; you need to be ready to put your money where your mouth is. Your inability to do this would make your efforts to be seen "as hypocritical or as 'woke-washing.'"

- *Will your constituencies agree with speaking out?*

You should ensure that your *key* constituencies are on your side, else you risk losing future businesses. In a case where your constituencies disagree, you must discuss and carefully analyze their relative importance to your company.

To provide a framework to guide a company's response to these questions, Argenti gave an instance using Starbucks. In 2018, a Philadelphia store manager of the company called the police after two Black men who were denied access to the bathroom refused to leave the store, which resulted in their arrest. After protests and online outrage, Starbucks apologized, issued a new bathroom policy, and shut down 8,000 stores for an afternoon of anti-bias training. According to Argenti, Starbucks' response checked yes for all three questions.

One, the issue aligned with Starbucks' strategy. In its mission, the company describes itself as "a third-place environment, where everyone is welcome, and we can gather, as a community, to share great coffee and deepen human connection." Hence, all customers must feel comfortable irrespective of race. Two, the company had the capacity to influence the issue. The anti-bias training, which instructed 175,000 baristas, was a medium to influence and ensure that people of color are treated well in the retail stores. Also, by shutting down 8,000 stores for the training, the coffee company demonstrated its commitment to the issue. Three, Starbucks's key constituencies—customers and community members—were outraged by the incident and supported Starbucks's response.[10]

The primary objective of Starbucks was to solve the issue of racial discrimination in its retail stores. However, it suffices to say that their response would appeal to people of color, and through that, they would gain more patronage. Solving a sensitive issue with such an approach would distinguish them from their competitors, especially if their competitors have never shown concern for any social issue.

- **The economic climate.** An entrepreneur can use a harsh economic climate to their advantage. It is logical for business people to protect their money in times of economic adversity, but is that always the smart decision? A harsh economic climate can be an indirect army for a company's growth and success. A perfect example of this was the coronavirus pandemic. In the cryptocurrency industry, some people speculated that the peak of the pandemic was a wrong time to invest in the digital asset, Bitcoin. Many people sold off their Bitcoin, crashing Bitcoin's price from about $10,312 in mid-February to $4,970 in mid-March.[11] But when people were selling off, smart investors were buying massively—using the rough economic weather to their advantage. And by December 2020, the same Bitcoin that people lost trust in rose to more than $23,000 (and is still rising as at the time of writing this). Those who sold regretted their actions, those who bought celebrated big wins. That is the benefit of using the economic climate as an indirect army.

When using an indirect army, be subtle. Use what I call "The Unpredictable Maneuver." I will elaborate on this strategy in chapter 7.

Let the competition be chaotic when you are calm, disorderly when you are organized, and weak when you are strong. Vu stated that "order or disorder is a product of the level of organization. Cowardice or courage is a product of position. Strength or weakness is a product of formation."

Your company will be orderly if your organizational level is excellent, courageous if you position yourself to take advantage of economic adversity, and strong if you form a tenacious army. A tenacious direct army will readily spot and employ an indirect army even without you urging them to. This is why you need to select smart, talented hands as members of your team. In Vu's words, choose talented subordinates that can create an advantage position.

Pledge to Action

I affirm that:

I have the right team.

I have a direct and indirect army that will always put my business ahead of the competition.

I will take advantage of technological advancements.

I am smart enough to have innovations that will put me miles ahead of the competition.

I am smart enough to take advantage of the sociopolitical climate and add value to society and my company.

I will not be anxious about harsh economic climates.

I understand that there are opportunities in every bad situation.

And I am prepared to seize these opportunities.

I will build the right team.

I will have the winning team.

CHAPTER SIX

The Early Bird

"Always attack. Even in defense, attack. The attacking arm possesses the initiative and thus commands the action. To attack makes men brave; to defend makes them timorous."

— Steven Pressfield

S trike while the iron is hot" is an old saying, but the value of its message has never been lost. When it comes to establishing a business, you have no time to waste. Once the business idea comes to you, start immediately (after you have drafted your plan). As an entrepreneur, nothing is more rewarding than starting early in your chosen niche. Sun Vu wrote: "As a general principle, the troops that arrive first at the location of the battle and wait for the enemy will have initiative and will be at ease. The troops that arrive later to the battle position will be passive and exhausted."

The world does not wait for anybody, and unless you are a psychic, you cannot tell for sure what the economic or sociopolitical climate will be in the future and how it can impact your business. I have come up with four important reasons that should motivate you to strike while the iron is hot.

Reasons why you need to launch your business idea immediately

Market saturation

As I stated in the first chapter of this book, human minds are soils and one idea can be deposited into different minds simultaneously. The more you delay launching your business, the more populated and saturated the market becomes, and the less market share you'll get. People who arrive early in an industry have the advantage of grabbing a sizable chunk of the market before the industry becomes saturated. Let's say you had an idea to launch a social media app in 2008, but you deferred this idea till 2020. Do you think you would be able to compete favorably in a market with social media heavyweights like Facebook, Twitter, Instagram, WhatsApp, LinkedIn, YouTube, Pinterest, Reddit, TikTok, and a host of others? For you to compete favorably, you must bring something different to the table, just like TikTok did.

TikTok was launched in 2016—twelve years and ten years after Facebook and Twitter, respectively—yet it got a sizable portion of the social media industry because of what it offered users. TikTok did not just offer its users a chance to create videos (YouTube had already given the world that); it gave them more. About TikTok and its unique selling point, Gary Vaynerchuk wrote: "TikTok provides a framework that makes it easier for people to create—especially if they don't know what else to do.

TikTok is making it easier for them to become content creators. It 1) allows them to create content that they would not otherwise be able to make as easily on their own, and 2) gives them a framework they can play or create within. For example, the TikTok app gives people tools like filters, control over video speed, access to professional audio and more. Even if you're not the best lip-syncer, you can still create something fun on TikTok with a music background."[1]

So unless you can offer users what they have not been offered before, you may not do well if you delay launching your business. Bringing something new to the industry is an idea, and mind you, you are not the only one with that idea. Extant and prospective companies may have the same idea. Just like you are studying and researching the current needs of the market, other companies are also doing the same. They are seeing what you are seeing, hearing what you are hearing. This is why you do not need to delay. You do not have the monopoly of an idea.

Evolution of trends

Chapter one took us through the different types of trends a business can align itself with. But it is important to reiterate that no trend lasts forever. Even a disruptive trend evolves. This gives you, the entrepreneur, another reason why you need to launch your business early.

Sometimes, if not most, business ideas come to us from what we perceive in our physical, social, economic, or political environment. And our perception is a product of the *current* happenings or trends in any of these environments. Thus, a business idea may only fit into a particular trend. Once that trend is gone, the idea may lose relevance if it does not evolve. We will see how a business idea can lose relevance later in this chapter.

Studying the terrain and launching more attacks

By coming into an industry early, you have the opportunity of studying the terrain before it gets crowded, and make plans towards scaling your business. It is more difficult to spot opportunities in a crowded place. There is a whole lot of noise to distract you. In a less crowded marketplace, you'd be able to spot gaps that need filling. Conversely, foresight and creativity would not be paramount objectives if you are coming into an already crowded space—a space where your competition had already filled the gaps you had intended to fill. Thus, your main concern would be how to get a portion of the market share —the crumbs from the table.

Same seed, diverse soils

I have mentioned this earlier. You do not have an exclusive right to an idea unless you implement it. As long as an idea is still cooling off in your mind, expect to see it being brought to life by another who is readier and more willing than you are. An idea is not yours for keeps. Inspiration can be deposited in *any fertile* mind. So when you receive an idea, always bear in mind that at least a hundred people have received the same idea.

Despite these important reasons for starting a business early, many business ideas have failed to blossom because the owners of these ideas were not willing to take action. And two factors cause this unwillingness: fear and doubt.

- **Fear.** We have heard countless times that fear means false evidence appearing real. After drafting out a plan, some prospective entrepreneurs would become scared of their vision. They become scared of the market or industry, of existing competition, of the perception of others. They feel that the vision is too big for them to achieve or that the idea is laughable. Then they grow cold feet and remain in their comfort zones.

Fear has not only killed prospective businesses, it has also killed existing businesses. Fear has crept into the mind of business owners because of setbacks they faced in the past. I once had a story of a man who invested about 10,000 dollars in bitcoin. Then bitcoin dropped so much in value, which made the man lose his investment. Since then, he has never dared to invest in cryptocurrency even though the industry's resilience has been proven over time.

For you to have a setback as an entrepreneur, it only means one thing: you're making progress. And that is why a challenge is trying to draw you back. Challenges, as we all know, are a part of life. But after you've been drawn back, do not forget that you were on a journey, on a mission to offer value to the world.

Fear raises a false alarm—it tells you that things would always go wrong. But the truth is if you can overcome your fear and forge ahead, you would discover that what you feared did not even exist. So always be courageous so that you would not miss out on the rewards of your vision.

- **Doubt.** For other entrepreneurs, they do not suffer from fear but doubt. They doubt the potentials in their vision. They doubt their ability to bring the vision to life. They doubt their encouragers and believe the lies of their naysayers. Most times, people fall into the trap of doubt when they focus only on the big picture.

I know that many motivational speakers keep admonishing people to look at the big picture. It is good advice. But there is a clause they usually leave out. Before you can get the picture, you have to fit smaller pictures together. The big picture can be overwhelming. Looking at the big picture alone would make you doubt your capacity to achieve it. However, simplifying your vision into smaller goals and objectives would inject you with renewed zeal. Seeing yourself achieving these smaller goals would build up your confidence that you can achieve the big one.

Do not wait till everything is perfect before you launch your idea. Sun Vu pointed out that "if we wait to gather forces with adequate equipment before attempting to take advantage, we risk coming too late." However, we must also strike a balance. Do not, in a bid to arrive early, ignore adequate preparation. Ensure you have the needed resources to start with; resources that would satisfy your client even as a beginner; resources you can scale later on. If this is not done and you hurry to abandon the needed resources because you want to take advantage, you risk losing the abandoned resources.

Arrive early with just the right amount of everything you need. Do not delay yourself because you are waiting for more. Heed the words of James Clear, who rightly remarked: "Rome wasn't built in a day, but they were laying bricks every hour. You don't have to do it all today. Just lay a brick. That's how you build an empire."

The entrepreneur must eschew fear and doubt—they are two principal factors that delay success. Sun Vu stated that delay in combat would make the weapons rust and the soldiers lose their morale. This also applies to the entrepreneur, but unfortunately, many entrepreneurs do not consider the impact of delay on their business.

Do not let your weapons rust

Weapons signify ideas. Every idea has a timeline. And when you delay in implementing an idea, it "rusts." Rusting can happen in two ways: (1) The idea loses relevance. (2) Another person gets and implements the idea.

How can an idea lose relevance?

The earth is in constant motion, and as it rotates, developments happen. Every new development in the world requires innovation. And every innovation starts with an idea. When innovation is not birthed at the right time, a new development comes into play and phases out the old one alongside the innovation it would have thrived on.

Let's take, for example, the days of the Walkman. The Walkman was a portable media player manufactured in the late 70s by Sony. Music lovers could easily slot in an audio cassette into the device and listen to songs as they walked through the streets. Now imagine this: If Sony had delayed in manufacturing the product and decided to defer it by three to four decades, do you think they would have had a market for the product in this era of Apple Music, Audiomack, and Airpods? Definitely not. The idea of a Walkman has become an obsolete and rusty one. During the heydays of the Walkman (1979 – 2010), Sony sold over 400 million units of Walkman portable players for about $150 per unit.[2] Now, if we ignore inflation and other market forces, it means that within 30 years, the company made over $60 billion. Sony would have lost this revenue if they had delayed their idea. Also, if they had delayed their innovation, there is the possibility of another company producing the same device. This is the second way a weapon can get rusty.

Life abhors vacuum. Many things in life are not indispensable or irreplaceable. It is in the nature of life to always balance itself. Ideas are like seeds, and the human mind is a soil. So, nature does not just deposit a seed—an idea—in the mind of one person alone. It disperses the seed so that if a particular soil delays the seed's sprouting, there would be two or three other soil types that would favor the seed's growth. The story of Blackberry comes to mind.

Alexandra Appolonia, in an article for *Business Insider*, noted that at one time, Blackberry had 50 percent of the smartphone market in the US, and 20 percent globally.[3] But the company met its death because it was slow to change, while another company, Apple, was receptive to change. Blackberry held on to its old designs of QWERTY keyboards, while Apple launched iPhones without keyboards. By the time they wanted to get onboard the innovation, it was already too late.[4] Controlling a major share of the smartphone market should have made Blackberry flexible and receptive to ideas, but this wasn't so. The ideas that were meant to thrive on the soil of the then king of smartphones, thrived better on iPhones. Other phone companies now aspired to produce iPhone-esque phones, while Blackberry faded into history.

I wonder what went through the minds of Blackberry's staff as they watched the company's steady decline. It is possible that some of the staff would have suggested that the company go with the trend, but their suggestions were discarded. Many staff would have lost their zeal as they watched the company's steady descent into irrelevance.

Do not let your soldiers lose morale

You cannot run your company on your energy and drive alone; you need the fire of and in your team. This is why you should never let them lose zeal. Keep them motivated at all times. And one of the most veritable ways to do this is by executing ideas as soon as they are birthed. Everyone wants to be part of a success story. By executing your ideas and winning through them, you give your team a sense of fulfillment. You allow them to explore their creativity, and the results of their creativity would make them hunger for more wins. They would want to replicate their success over and over again.

If you keep deferring the execution of your ideas, soon your team would lose faith in you. Fear, doubt, and laziness are perceptible. Your staff can tell if you are afraid, doubtful, or just lazy. Once they notice any of these, they would stick with you just for their remunerations, not because they are motivated to work.

A demotivated team is a weakness and a threat to a company. Like Sun Vu said, if the enemy discovers this weakness, then an attack would be inevitable. It is easy for a rival company to poach a demotivated staff. And such staff wouldn't mind revealing the business secrets to their new company. This is one method through which an unexecuted idea is transferred to the next soil.

In a LinkedIn article, Victoria Ahl shared four stories of how different companies cleverly poached talent from rival companies. Two out of these four stories stand out for me. First is the story of MediConnect Global. The company bought an old truck and turned it into a mobile hiring center. They would park at the competitor's parking lot and hand out flyers to people walking by during lunchtime. The strategy worked. What was striking for me was what the CEO, Amy Rees Anderson, said when she recounted the experience to *Forbes*. She said that the ploy ended up being incredibly successful for her company. It engaged current employees, endeared them to the business, and *increased their sense of company pride.*"[5]

When a worker seeks company pride in another company, it means that that worker is no longer happy in their current company. Such a worker wants a fresh challenge and new wins, which the current company no longer offers because of reasons like failing to execute ideas.

A similar event occurred between Snapchat and Uber. A few years ago, Uber employees at their San Francisco office noticed a geo-specific Snapchat filter. The filter had the question, "This place is driving you mad?" and also had images of wayward taxis crowding the bottom of the screen, alongside a link to Snapchat's career page.[6] If an Uber staff clicked the link, it meant one thing: the company, Uber, was actually driving the staff mad.

Keeping your team motivated is very important. You should understand that you've got a bundle of talents working with you. Rival companies know that your success is tied greatly to your staff, so they desire what you have got. If they perceive a whiff of demotivation, they will do anything to keep the bundle of talents to themselves.

When you allow your team to be poached by the competition, the competition has used one of Sun Vu's many tactics on you. Vu stated that because of the cost of war, a wise general should forage and feed his troops with the enemy's food supplies. He wrote that "eating one "bushel" of enemy's food will save us the rigor of bringing along twenty." This is the mindset of your competition. It would save them both time and financial resources to poach talent from your company than carrying out a recruitment process to find that talent. Don't allow yourself to be played. Don't allow another company to strengthen itself with your human resources. So, motivate your team *always*.

A good way to keep your team motivated is by reiterating Sun Vu's words to them: "Anger must be the impetus to destroy the enemy and reward must be the stimulus to defeat the enemy." What is the enemy? Lack, financial stress, poverty. You should not be the only one motivated by the desire for financial freedom. This desire should be in every member of your team. They should understand that the company's success puts them a step ahead in their journey to financial liberation.

Let them be driven by the anger and frustration that comes with lack, with having a need and lacking the capacity to meet it. Let this anger drive them to provide value to their community and the world at large. Know this: There is wealth in this world, but it can only be accessed by those who offer value. It is an exchange system: give value, receive wealth.

While motivated by this anger, they should also balance and consolidate their passion with the knowledge of the reward they would receive at the end. Apart from the financial reward, let them think of the sense of fulfillment that comes with the knowledge that they were part of a creative process that offered immense value to the world.

You worked hard to get your team to believe in your vision, so do all it takes to sustain the fire. If you do not, you may lose them, and when you do, you may never get them to believe (in) you again. You don't want this happening.

Pledge to Action

I affirm that:

I am not just a talker but a doer.

I am not just a dreamer but an achiever.

I understand that nature hates vacuum, so I wouldn't willingly allow my ideas to be taken because I refused to act.

I do away with fear.

I do away with doubt.

I am a brave.

I have faith in my vision.

My vision is powerful and I cannot wait to show it to the world.

My team would not lose motivation because of me.

They will be ever-motivated and focused because they look up to me.

I spot ideas and act on them quickly.

I am the early bird.

CHAPTER SEVEN

The Unpredictable Maneuver

"Others follow patterns; we alone are unpredictable."

— Mignon McLaughlin

D o not let your competition know that you are not in line with their thoughts. Leaning on the ideas of Sun Vu, this is what I term "The Unpredictable Maneuver."

Vu stated that maneuvering is the most difficult task in warfare. According to him, it involves turning a curved situation into a straight one and disadvantages into advantages. And you have to do this without the enemy being aware. You have to be subtle. Unpredictable.

When there is chaos, act as if you are also affected by the chaos. This is what Sun Vu meant when he wrote: "In the chaotic situation of the battle, our army may seem to be in chaos, but in reality, we cannot be chaotic. In a chaotic and tangled situation, the distribution of our troops may seem disorderly, but in reality, it is invisible. In this way, chaos clearly masks for real organization, cowardice masks for courage, weak force masks for strong force."

There are some points you need to take note of when employing unpredictable maneuvering. These points as outlined by Sun Vu include:

- **Victory belongs to the person who masters the combination of curvature and straightness.** Understand that in business, the path will not always be straight. Curves and bumps are bound to exist. Navigating these curves should not translate into a loss and a depressing moment for you. Learn to use these curves to your advantage. Let them be tools for your victory.

- **In battle, human voices are not strong enough to be heard, which is why we use gongs and trumpets. Our vision is not accurate enough, which is why we use banners and flags**. It is the same in business; you cannot attract attention to yourself through your voice alone. This is why you need effective marketing skills to amplify your voice. However, in this case of unpredictable maneuvering, you have to go beyond conventional marketing. In times of chaos, you have to get your customers to be your gongs and trumpets. And you would need to do this subtly. We can cite an example with the coronavirus pandemic. It was a moment of chaos. Everybody was physically and psychologically drained by fear. It was not the best of moments for companies to advertise their businesses, especially using the virus as a tool to promote their products. A bar in New Zealand came under fire for doing this. Their ad showed an image of two men in boiler suits and gas masks, each holding a bottle of Corona beer. The image had the caption: "CATCH SOME CORONA AT HOUSE THIS SUMMER."[1] It was a tacky promotion. Unfortunately, the bar did not see anything wrong with the ad.[2] It was a wordplay intended for humor, but it came at the wrong time. As at the time the promotion was released, over 360 people had died of the virus in Asia, and there were nearly 18,000 cases globally.[3] It was not a time for jokes. If the bar wanted to stay ahead of their competitors in a moment of chaos, I think they failed at it. It was a poor attempt at unpredictable maneuvering.

However, there were companies that employed unpredictable maneuvering effectively. For example, Coursera offered free courses to universities worldwide during the pandemic,[4] LinkedIn opened up 16 of its learning courses for free,[5] Dolce & Gabbana partnered with the Humanitas University to fund a coronavirus research project, and Giorgio Armani donated $1.43 million to four hospitals in Rome and Milan, as well as to the Civil Protection Agency.[6] The actions of these companies were unpredictable maneuvering at its best. They used empathy as their gongs and trumpets to amplify their voices, and charity as their flags and banners to demonstrate their vision and values[7]. These actions would leave an indelible mark on their beneficiaries, and these beneficiaries would love to be associated with these brands even beyond Covid-19.

- **Snatch away the morale of the enemy.** Always make the competition doubt their capacity. And the only way to do this is by getting the people on your side. While the competition is giving people what they want, give the people what they *need*. Once you give people what they need, you get them on your side and take away the enemy's morale. This was the case between Apple and Blackberry. Blackberry was busy riding on the wings of its elite status coupled with its popularity and multimillion-dollar deals and failed to innovate. Then Apple came with its keyboard-less iPhones, which were updated every year. Other smartphones copied iPhone's model, and Blackberry couldn't just keep up. Their morale was deflated— completely flattened.

Sun Vu pointed out that, "When an army first arrives at the scene, their morale is sharp and strong, after a while it becomes languid and lazy, and finally wants to return home." A similar scenario occurs in business. For some businesses, their morale tapers. They get comfortable with their current status and their current market share. They slack on their company culture; they stop aiming to become better. This was Blackberry's undoing, and iPhone capitalized on the opportunity to take over the smartphone market. Sun Vu advised the general to fight when the enemy's morale is low. While this may be a good strategy for warfare, it may not be completely healthy in business. Remember, we have emphasized so much on timing. Start early. Don't wait for the enemy's morale to get low before you strike. (What if the morale doesn't get low?) Take away the morale by intimidating the competition with your innovation.

- **Do not approach to fight with the enemy troops on a high hill.** Know your level. Fight at your level. Before competing against another company in your industry, make sure you are on the same level with them in finance, quality of human resources, and/or innovative ideas. You cannot be a newbie in an industry and decide to compete with industry giants. You can only aspire to be a giant, then become a giant, before competing with giants. In the world of smartphones, some names first come to mind before others. Apple and Samsung. Then others. These two companies are miles ahead of others in terms of market share, company valuation, quality of human resources, and innovation. Other phone companies like Huawei, Ericsson, and Nokia mainly compete among themselves.

As an entrepreneur, know your league. Knowing your league doesn't mean you wouldn't aspire to play in a bigger league. All I am saying is that you should not burn resources competing against companies that have the resources more than you. Bigger companies have the resources and know-how to create a lot of touchpoints. Say you are a new telephone company how would you compete with Apple's over twenty touchpoints—including their packaging, a clean website, store locations, personal set-up, software development kits, questionnaires on satisfaction, and number of employees?[8] It would be practically impossible to beat that at your level.

- **Do not press too hard with a desperate troop.** Never be the desperate company. The market is wide enough for everybody. All you need is patience. Desperation would lead you to make mistakes that may soil your company's reputation. Jeff Wiener shared a story of how a company, desperate to beat his company, resorted to copying everything Jeff's company did. The company copied their blogposts and primary web pages (including the typos). The only thing they changed was the company name. They even left the name of Jeff's company in their meta description and meta keywords.[9] That is how desperate they were.

Desperation will only hurt you *if you allow it to consume you*. I put that caveat because desperation helped a company like Nike. In an act of desperation to gain a competitive edge over Reebok, Nike signed Michael Jordan[10]—a deal that revolutionized the company. In 2019, the company made $3.14 billion from the Nike Air Jordan brand.[11] If you want to be desperate, then make healthy decisions.

Don't be reckless. Don't take unnecessary risks. Don't overwork your team just because you want them to meet up. You will only dampen their morale if you do that. Do not be the desperate one. Let the competition be the desperate company, then use their desperation to your advantage. Quoting Lior Arussy, Vivian Giang wrote in her *Forbes* article: "People do a lot of stupid things when they're desperate and if you can understand their level of confidence, you can exploit their weaknesses."[12]

Vivian also advised that entrepreneurs should figure out what makes the competition desperate and become exceptional at what the competition lacks. "For example, if they are lacking in customer service, deliver an authentic and personalized experience to your own customers. If you're a smaller company, send your customers birthday cards and personalized letters," she wrote.[13]

A successful entrepreneur is one that is flexible and able to turn challenges into bright prospects. The competition will always be eager to know what's up his sleeves. That is the entrepreneur you should become. When the market or other uncontrollable factors take everyone by surprise, catch your breath and think out how to maneuver the challenge. Let your maneuver be smooth and subtle.

Pledge to Action

I affirm that:

I see opportunities and take advantage of them.

I will use challenges as raw materials for my success.

I am a master of curves and straights.

Therefore, I will not be caught unawares.

With my innovation, I will take away the morale of the enemy.

I am calm.

I am collected.

I am not desperate.

I know desperation would lead to mistakes.

And I don't need to make any mistakes while I engage the unpredictable maneuver.

CHAPTER EIGHT

The Contingencies

"One thing that makes it possible to be an optimist is if you have a contingency plan for when all hell breaks loose."

— Randy Pausch

You may get everything right in your business—from planning to building your team to outpacing your competition—yet things would still go wrong. And it may likely be no fault of yours or your team. As humans, the only element of time we have full control of is the present. We can only predict the future; we cannot control it.

As a smart entrepreneur, it is important you prepare yourself for these contingencies. Do not be caught off-guard. Understand that these unforeseen events are bound to happen. This means that you should make provisions for them in your plan. Always ask yourself: What if this happens, what will I do? This does not mean you are a pessimist. On the contrary, it makes you a realist. You understand that it is in the nature of life to throw surprises at us once in a while.

Your ability to navigate unexpected challenges lies in your preparedness. Build your capacity. Have a high adversity quotient (I will discuss this later in this chapter).

Sun Vu advised the general to be prepared for changes that may happen on the battlefield. He didn't just inform the general of the likely events that may occur, he also taught the general what to do. And his lessons can also apply to you as an entrepreneur.

The Five Contingency Lessons from Sun Vu

Lesson 1: *If the terrain is not favorable, the force must not be stationed.*

One of the fundamental problems of the average human is the resistance to change. The average human would not want to take no for answer even when a yes may be detrimental. This should not be your story as an entrepreneur. As you draft out your plans on the drawing board, bear in mind that the real-life conditions for the business may not be favorable for you. Be open-minded enough to understand and *accept* this.

"If the *terrain* is not favorable, do not station your force." Terrain in this context is different from the types of terrain we saw in chapter one. The terrain in this context is *the* integral factor of the business. That factor is *you*.

You are the terrain. And yes, you can be unfavorable to your business. This may brew confusion in your mind, but hang in there. I know I have told you that you are the main repository of your vision. However, you should understand that things may be wrong with you. You may be toxic to your own vision. Don't forget you are a soil too, just like every other human being. And not all soils support every seed.

The good thing about starting a business is that it reveals qualities about you that you never knew existed. It takes you through a growth process. So you may have drafted your plans and when it is time to take action you discover certain traits about yourself that may be detrimental to your vision. Once this happens, do not station your force. Do not start the business.

What traits would you discover?

You may harbor a *lot* of traits that can be the little foxes that destroy the vine. In fact, Daphne Blake lists up to 100 of these traits. But according to Blake, these 100 traits can be grouped into eight major traits.[1] For each trait, I have listed certain questions you should use to assess if you possess any of the traits.

- *You are not cut out for entrepreneurship*

    - Am I motivated by money?

    - Am I motivated by fame?

    - Am I starting the business to escape from something?

    - Do I avoid difficult conversations?

    - Have I burnt all my bridges?

    - Am I confident and disciplined?

    - Do I know my strengths and weaknesses?

    - Do I have a vision for the future?

    - Can I accept and handle the possibility of failure?

    - Am I passionate about this business?

- *You are not in the right place in your life*

    - Am I caring for young children or aging relatives?

    - Do I have weak support systems?

    - Do I have other engagements (e.g., schoolwork) that I need to commit to?

    - Do I have physical or mental health challenges that would affect my work?

    - Will my business affect my emotional/romantic relationship?

- Can I give up sleep to get the work done?

- Do I have a free time in my schedule?

- Do I have the opportunity to travel?

- Do I have good outlets for stress?

- Am I willing to give up my hobbies?

- *You have a personality problem*

  - Do I want or love routine?

  - Do I hate networking and motivating others?

  - Do I always want to be in control?

  - Do I lack focus and organization?

  - Am I obsessed with perfection and hate being wrong?

  - Am I creative?

  - Can I handle failure?

  - Am I given to learning?

  - Can I self-evaluate?

  - Can I complete projects?

- *Your finances are not in order*

  - Do I have a low credit score?

  - Am I in debt?

  - Do I have huge financial obligations?

  - Do I need a steady salary to survive?

- Am I totally dependent on bank loans to start my business?

- Do I have a budget?

- Do I have other funding plans aside from venture capital or angel investors?

- Do I understand that crowdfunding may not be successful?

- Do I have an insurance plan?

- Do I have a backup plan?

- *You have a faulty business idea*

  - Am I in love with my idea that I cannot let it go even when it is not feasible?

  - Am I scared to tell others my idea because they will reveal its weaknesses?

  - Am I starting this business because a friend or relative is into it?

  - Is my idea devoid of innovation?

  - Do I lack the resources to bring my vision to life?

  - Do I understand how my idea can be profitable?

  - Do I have a compelling business proposition?

  - Have I done a pre-launch market testing to ascertain the demand for my offering?

  - Can I withstand the competition in the market?

- Do I understand the market or industry I am getting into?

- *You don't know what you are doing*

    - Do I hate customer service?

    - Do I hate data and analyzing them?

    - Will I be uncomfortable firing underperforming staff?

    - Do I have a problem scaling a business?

    - Do I have a wrong definition of success?

    - Do I understand how entrepreneurship works?

    - Do I know how to delegate duties?

    - Do I know how to recruit staff and set KPIs?

    - Do I understand cash flow?

    - Do I know how to value and price my products?

Assessment Guide 1: *For you to be an entrepreneur, your answers to the first 5 questions should be negative, while the remaining 5 should be positive. If your score is less than 60%, then you are not cut out for entrepreneurship.*

- *You don't know how to sell*

    - Do I know how to attract customers?

    - Do I understand the difference between features and benefits?

    - Can I give a compelling value proposition?

    - Do I listen to my customers?

- Can I sell my vision to mentors, investors, and stakeholders?

- Can I get a partner or co-founder on board?

- Can I motivate my team?

- *You can't handle risk*

  - Can I handle uncertainty and surprises?

  - Do I know how to manage and minimize risks?

  - Do I have mentors?

  - Do I have a plan for handling lawsuits and negative press?

Assessment Guide 2: *For you to be an entrepreneur, your answers to all the questions above should be positive. If your score is less than 60%, then you are not cut out for entrepreneurship.*

Provide honest answers to these questions. And once you see that you do not have what it takes to be an entrepreneur, once you see the terrain is not favorable, do not deploy forces. Retreat. Get things right. Then try again.

Lesson 2: *Do not linger on a barren land.*

Sayings like "Never give up" and "Winners don't quit. Quitters don't win" have made many remain in businesses that are not profitable. Your decision to leave an unprofitable business is *solely* at your discretion. I say this because there are popular businesses that are not making profit yet are still in business. Examples include Snap Inc., Uber, Lyft, Airbnb, Dropbox, Soundcloud, YouTube, and others.[2]

The question that may be going through your mind is this: *If these companies aren't profitable and are still in business, why should I close shop*? Know this: These companies are still in business because they make revenue and are also backed by investors. They are global brands. They add value to their customers. The only issue is that the business doesn't give them any profit to enjoy. Now, we cannot term these brands barren. They witness *consistent* growth.

- Does your business experience consistent growth?

- Are you making enough sales to cover the operations of the company?

- Is the business sustaining itself without your personal funds?

- Are you still physically and mentally fit in spite of the demands of the business?

- Are your key employees still with you?

- Are customers (still) impressed with your product?

Your honest answers to these questions will tell you if you are wasting time on a barren land or not. If you gave a negative answer to more than 60% of these questions, then you are lingering on a barren land. Move.

Lesson 3: *If besieged, you have to think straight.*

One of the questions asked in Lesson 1 was: "Do I have physical or mental health challenges that would affect my work?" This question is vital because you need to be physically and mentally alert in times of unexpected drastic events. A wrong decision made in a moment of panic can ruin your entire business.

Events like lawsuits, natural disasters, and fire outbreaks can be a heavy blow to your belly. They can make you lose air . You see everything you've worked for (almost) destroyed in a wink.

These moments are tough. Sometimes these moments would determine the life or death of your business. Sun Vu advised that in moments of life and death, you have to take risks. But be careful not to make any hasty decisions—take calculated risks.

You have to maintain composure and grit for yourself, your team, and your customers. In his article for *Life Hack*, Tanvir Zafar noted that to defy existential crises as an entrepreneur, you have to understand your purpose for being in business in the first place. It is this understanding, this conviction in your identity, that will help you withstand challenges.[3] Zafar echoed the words of Christian T. Russell, the president of Dangerous Tactics: "You have to know your purpose for running your company in the first place! Why does your business exist? Who do you serve? What do they need most from you, right now? 99% of business owners do not take the time for this introspection."[4]

Be part of the 1% of business owners that have time for this introspection. Your challenge shouldn't be the end of your business.

Lesson 4: *There are roads you should not cross.*

There are different routes to a destination, but depending on your position, you must not go through every route. In good times, in times where your mind is not muddled by unexpected events, it is easy to know and choose the routes to follow. However, when you become anxious due to events that take you by surprise, you may take the wrong routes.

There are two roads you should not take in times of anxiety and uncertainty. They are: The Road of Impatience and The Road of Non-delegation. These two roads may seem appealing, but they may be detrimental to your business.

The Road of Impatience. When unexpected events happen, we want to get out of them as soon as possible. And we may want to take the quick route, even when it is not the right route. This is why you need to have a high adversity quotient. Adversity quotient measures your ability to withstand challenges without breaking. Impatience or haste is the extra force that pushes you to your breaking point. But if you can withstand just a little more, you will get the logical and perfect solution to the challenge. No matter what happens, follow through the process. You will see the light at the end.

The Road of Non-delegation. In times of adversity, we lose trust in people, in our team. We feel that it's because we didn't do something right that's why things went wrong. So, in seeking a solution to the challenge, we would want to handle everything ourselves because we don't want things to go wrong again. This may seem understandable, but it is unhealthy. During the times of challenges, that is when you need to do two important things: *seek help* and *release control*. It is a time you need all the help you can get. It is a time you need to consider other perspectives. It is a time to delegate tasks. Surround yourself with think-tanks, mentors, and trusted employees who are committed to ensuring that things become normal again.

Lesson 5: *We sometimes do not fight the enemy*

This may seem like a contradiction, but it is ideal. The enemy here is your competition. And there are times when you don't fight the enemy. There are times you need to collaborate with the enemy, because the enemy may have what you need. Perrie Kapernaros noted that competitive collaboration is a "healthy and viable" road to take in your business.[5]

This corroborates what I stated earlier about an entrepreneur not taking the road to non-delegation. You cannot do it all alone. And sometimes, your best allies would be your competition. We see, or we've seen excellent competitive collaboration in Microsoft and Intel, Pfizer and Merck, Vimeo and YouTube[6], even Samsung and Apple (Samsung supplies screens to Apple).[7]

Before you fight the enemy, think of collaboration—because, according to Kapernaros, it can help you increase profits, improve brand awareness, and attract your target market.

These are the likely unexpected events you may encounter in the battlefield of business. Asides these five events, there are also five mistakes or drawbacks you must avoid. When you handle unexpected events well enough and go ahead to avoid these mistakes, you set yourself on a path to become a successful, well-rounded entrepreneur.

The Five Dangerous Drawbacks

"Recklessness, greed, anger, self-conceit, a men pleaser. These five are common mistakes and catastrophes to the successful conduct of the war." - Sun Vu

Throughout this book, I have given you strategies for success in business. The strategies are not foolproof. Did I shock you with that statement? Of course, they are not foolproof because of one factor: you. You are human—an emotional being. And your emotions can interfere with these strategies and mar them. A human being has a total of 27 emotions.[8] Therefore, it is impossible to apply these strategies without interference from your emotions. For example, in chapter six, I highlighted how *fear*, a human emotion, can limit you from launching your business on time. Apart from fear, Sun Vu listed five dangerous emotions or traits that can drastically affect your business. But before we look at these emotions or traits, we will look at an overview of emotions—what they are and how they differ from feelings.

What are emotions?

Simply put, emotions are involuntary responses to external or internal stimuli. Our body processes sensory information—sight, smell, sound, taste, and touch—received from our external environment. For instance, you are walking on a lonely path and you see a lion, you will feel afraid. You would tremble, your heart would beat faster, you would have a dry mouth, you would be mentally and physically alert to take flight. All these are your body's way of processing the information it received from your sense of sight. This means that emotions are physically expressed.

Not only does the body use emotions to process information from our external environment, it also uses them to process information received from our internal environment; our mind. Our mind, which is the seat of our memory and thoughts, can trigger an emotion. For example, if you lost a loved one, you would feel sad whenever you remember that person even a long time after their demise. That is the body using an emotion—sadness—to process internal information, a memory. Remember, emotions are involuntary; we have no control over them. No one chooses to be afraid when they sight a lion. No one chooses to be sad when they remember a dead loved one. These emotions overwhelm the human body because they are a product of physiological processes we have no control over. And this is where emotions differ from feelings.

Many often confuse emotions with feelings (and vice versa), but they are different, even though they are related. So, what are feelings?

Feelings are our reactions after we have processed and understood emotions. They are simply the feedback we give after an emotion. While emotions are physically expressed, feelings are mentally expressed. They counterbalance the physical responses we express as a result of our emotions. For instance, if you see a lion on a lonely street, you can choose not to *feel* threatened (although it would take a lot of courage to do that). Unlike the emotion, fear, which you could not control, you can control what you feel. Instead of feeling threatened, you can make the conscious effort of feeling calm. The same thing applies when you feel sad because you remembered a loved one. Instead of sadness, you can choose to feel happy, holding on to the belief that they are in a better place.

Emotions and feelings are often seen as the same because there is a quick switch from emotions to feelings. The line dividing the two is too thin that it is imperceptible. We often don't know when we have transited into feeling from emotions.

We have to understand the workings of emotions and feelings because the inability to neutralize a negative or inappropriate emotion with the right feeling may cost us a whole lot. Now, let us see the five emotions/traits/actions that can be catastrophic to your business.

❖ **Recklessness**

"Reckless disregard for death will actually lead to death." - Sun Vu

Entrepreneurship is all about risks. This risk stems from the inability to accurately know what the future holds. We go into entrepreneurship with a blend of predictions, history, and hope. The market dynamics are not subject to our dictates, thus we position ourselves according to the market dynamics, hoping that our position will favor us. If we can accurately know the future, then it would be easy for us to know what or what not to do. It is this uncertainty that makes business risky.

Now, some people have interpreted risk as recklessness. You'd hear them say things like, "Life is all about risk." This is true. But it is quite different for business. Business is not all about risk, but *calculated* risk. Just like Sun Vu said, if you interpret risk as recklessness, and have total disregard for the life of your business, then your business would definitely meet its end.

There are countless books and articles that tell motivating stories of people and/or businesses that took risks and succeeded. But there are hardly any stories of those who took risks and failed. These businesses went into oblivion and are not remembered because they mistook recklessness for risk.

The reason why people become reckless is that they cannot control an important emotion: excitement. The general who is reckless with his attack may be excited about his troops' strength or number, his weapons, his strategy, or the enemy's supposed weaknesses. The reckless businessman is excited about the prospect of huge profits to be made, his team's strength, financial acumen, or the competition's supposed weaknesses. This excitement strips off his thought process. He doesn't analyze the market. All he thinks about is taking action. Such a businessman is headed for doom. He would plow his resources into the venture, only for him to hit a brick wall. This is why you should avoid being reckless at all costs. Now, the question is, how do you do this? How do you know you are moving towards recklessness instead of (calculated) risk? To answer this question, I would borrow the ideas of Gwen Moran, a Business and Finance writer and author.

In an article for *Entrepreneur*, Moran outlined four traits for entrepreneurs —risk-takers—to watch out for. For me, these traits are signals that would alert you when you are crossing the thin line between risk and recklessness.

- **Sensation-seeking.** Some people become reckless because they love the adrenaline rush that accompanies recklessness. They are entrepreneurial daredevils. Moran stated that people who naturally crave sensation and seek out risky adventures like skydiving might transfer this trait into their business. They want to thrive where the atmosphere is chaotic or where they are engaged in high-stakes decision making.[9] If you are such a person, it is expedient you dampen this excitement and think things through before acting. Move beyond emotions and transcend into feelings. Although you are excited and pumped-up, choose to feel calm. Choose to be calculating. Choose to be analytical.

- **Unconcerned about consequences.** People who are unconcerned about consequences are the people to whom Sun Vu directed the saying, "Reckless disregard for death will actually lead to death." These businesspeople simply do not care about the outcome of their actions. And I wonder why this is so. If you wouldn't be bothered about the longevity of your business, why start up the business in the first place? Some erroneously define this unconcern as bravery. Being cautious is not cowardice. It only means you value your business and resources that you wouldn't want to jeopardize them. When you notice that you are unbothered about the outcomes of your risks, then you should know you are approaching recklessness. However, in the words of Moran, "That's not to say you should be paralyzed by fear, but you should understand what could happen if the outcome of your action or decision is not as you'd hoped and have an idea of what you'll do in that situation."[10]

- **Impulsiveness.** When you are about to take a risk, ask yourself: Did I think this through, or am I just being impulsive? You can get an answer to this question by analyzing past decisions you have taken. Is there a pattern? Do you fail to carry out adequate research each time you're to make a decision? Do you regret your actions later? These questions are necessary because, just as Moran noted, "People who have issues with willpower and who tend to make decisions quickly without doing the necessary research or investigation are typically more prone to making reckless decisions than those who are more disciplined."[11] Quoting Steven Mundahl, co-author of *The Alchemy of Authentic Leadership*, she added that such people are "the type of people who will follow a plan for a while, but then will throw it all away with a decision that looks good at the time instead of keeping the big picture in mind."[12] This tells you that a moment of impulsiveness can ruin everything you did at the drawing board.

- **Denial.** This is another trait to watch out for. Many reckless people fail to accept the reality of life. Sometimes, a reckless person knows they are reckless, but they keep believing a lie because of the anticipated reward. In Moran's words, "They prefer not to face the reality of their choices. Instead, they ignore fallout or make excuses for why a particular decision didn't work out. They also make light of the potential for failure or choose to disregard it entirely. People who have trouble facing a situation's facts are more likely to make decisions that are not grounded in the best interest of the company."[13]

These signals do not only prevent you from being reckless, they also help you ask the necessary questions for taking calculated risks. Questions like:

- Why do I want to do this?

- Is this actually good for my business, or am I just looking for a thrill?

- What are the possible outcomes of this decision?

- Is this venture sustainable?

- Does this venture have a solid roadmap?

- Am I unbothered about the consequences of my actions?

- Do I feel that this venture is foolproof and I do not need to think about it?

- Am I facing reality or shielding myself from it?

- Am I only motivated by prospective gains?

-   Do I love my vision so much as not to jeopardize it?

❖ Greed

"A greedy general will be captured." - Sun Vu

Greed is just as drastic as recklessness. In fact, greed is one of the causes of recklessness. Don't be a businessman that doesn't know when to stop. There is a difference between aspiring for more and being greedy. When you aspire for more, it means that you want to scale your business without losing sight of your vision and core values. It means that you want to grow based on what your business needs, not what you want. On the other hand, when you are greedy, you have the *excessive* desire to want more—even more than what your business needs.

Often, greed is a product of impatience. In a bid to rise quickly, some entrepreneurs seek and inject so much funds into their business and in the end, suffocate it. You may be wondering how this is possible. I hear you ask: "Thẩm, I thought funding is what every business needs to thrive?" That's true. But there is also the popular saying that too much of anything is bad. Anastasia Belyh explained three ways in which too much funding can be detrimental to a business.

First, too much funding, especially as a startup, will raise your company's valuation so high. While this may seem like a good thing, "gathering high valuations initially can lead to expectations that may be out of the reach of a company that has only just begun operations. Companies that are new market entrants might not have the market knowledge to achieve targets that come coupled with high value funding,"[14] Belyh wrote.

Second, driven by the desire to inject funds into your business, you may likely not be selective about the type of investors you want in your business. This would result in you having numerous investors, which would, in turn, affect your business. Belyh rightly pointed out that many investors are difficult to manage, thus it is better to have a few investors who understand your business than to have many whose ideologies do not align with yours. Belyh cited an example: "Let's say a small business has sixty investors (a large number for a small business) this means that when making decisions, the business proprietor will need to take into account sixty opinions and sixty expectations."[15]

Third, apart from having too many investors, having low-quality investors could also be detrimental to your business. Don't be so funds-driven that you do not care about the type of person(s) investing in your business. When all you are concerned about is who has the money, you would not care if they understand your company's mission, vision, unique selling proposition, and core values. For this reason, Belyh advised that your number of investors should be small and well informed because it cuts back the time it takes to explain menial things to the investors. She further added that: "When you are scanning and filtering investors for quality, choose those who have had experience investing in your respective industry. They can provide helpful information and explain some of the workings of the industry to new industry entrants."[16]

Grow your business based on what it needs and not based on your greed. Sun Vu said that the greedy general gets captured. When you are greedy, you become ensnared by the poverty you were trying to escape from. And Kayla Matthews noted that this could happen in 10 ways. I have highlighted 8 out of these 10 ways, which I consider too important to ignore.[17]

1. **You look for ways to make money, and not to improve.** This means that you sacrifice quality on the altar of an excessive desire for wealth. You forgo excellent customer experience. You are only concerned about cutting costs and gaining more wealth.

2. **You make bad personnel decisions.** You may overlook the flaws of your team members as long as they are making you money. Matthews stated that an employer might ignore sexual harassment perpetrated by one of his managers because that manager is his top salesman.

3. **You don't spend money making your employees happy.** If you are a greedy entrepreneur, not only would you be unconcerned about your customers, you would also be unconcerned about your employees. A business that cares less about its employees is a dead business already. In Matthews' words: "Happy employees make for good businesses, because they are the bridge between you and your customers. When employees are unhappy, they won't do their best for you, and that can actually lead to a decline in sales."

4. **You forego vacations to work.** In a bid to make more money, you are likely to burn yourself out. You would only be concerned with work, work, work. You might even make your team work without vacation—an action that can leave harmful consequences on your team. Greed would tell you the lie that you don't have the luxury of taking a break. It would tell you that while you're resting, your competitors are moving miles ahead of you. But as I said, these are all lies. You would need to take a break. If you do not take a break, then you'd break down. And that would likely end your business.

5. **You take on more clients than you can effectively manage.** You want all the money to yourself. So, you keep taking orders even when you know that

you are choked already. This will result in you delivering a shabby service, burning yourself out, and ultimately denting your business's image. Matthews put it better when she wrote: "If you stretch your staff too thin with your workload, [your] clients will not be happy with your work. Worse yet, word may leak out to other potential clients that you're not meeting deadlines or producing good work."

6. **You squander your clients' trust.** As a follow up to the previous point, when you keep delivering a shabby job or fail to meet up with clients' expectations, you'd lose their trust. Trust is a pillar that upholds your business, and once this pillar is gone, your business begins to collapse gradually. On the issue of trust, Matthews wrote: "When it becomes clear that you only care about making money, you risk losing even the most loyal clients. They want someone working for them who sees them as more than just a dollar sign."

7. **You alienate your employees.** A greedy employer would overwork his team, get them to make money for him, and then give them a remuneration not commensurate with their effort. This can deflate the morale of your team. And when this happens, they wouldn't mind selling you out to your competition.

8. **You're not mentoring anyone.** Many do not know this, but mentorship is vital for a business. Beyond money, mentorship helps you expand the value you add to the world. Your mentees become outgrowths of you. Steve Jobs mentored Mark Zuckerberg. Warren Buffett mentored Bill Gates. Christian Dior

mentored Yves Saint-Laurent.[18]   As a successful mentor, you would look at what your mentees have built and feel a sense of fulfillment that money cannot buy.   However, greed has the power of denying you this.   According to Matthews, many entrepreneurs nurse the thought that there is no monetary reward for mentoring, so they shove it aside.   But for Matthews, it is a foolish thought "because great mentors produce great workers who can carry on your business for years to come — and ultimately make you more money to boot."

Avoid greed. Be patient. Build gradually. Feed your business with only what it needs. And you'll definitely win. You'll see.

❖ Anger

"The angry general is easily provoked into taking superficial action." - Sun Vu

As an entrepreneur, it is almost impossible not to get angry at certain situations or people. Remember, anger is an emotion, and we cannot control emotions. Why would you get angry as an entrepreneur? The answer is simple: things will not always go your way. They wouldn't always go as you planned them. I stated earlier that entrepreneurship is all about history, prediction, hope, and patience. There are times when your predictions wouldn't be correct. It is normal to get angry and frustrated in those times, but you have to choose how to respond to the anger.

As an entrepreneur, there are five elements that you are likely to get angry at. They are life, your market/industry, your employees/team, your competition, and yourself.

- **Life**. It is often said that life doesn't give you what you deserve, but what you demand. But the process of

121

demanding often takes a long time. The process of making a demand on life is quite frustrating and exhausting. You begin to wish that life was a bit lenient. You wonder why things are not going as planned when you have done everything right on the drawing board. You have gotten sufficient capital. You have gotten the right team. You are innovative; you are confident in the quality of your product. Yet, for no fault of yours, things are just not working out. It is in times like this you feel like punching the wall or throwing a flower vase.

- **Your market/industry.** Sometimes, life may not be the culprit. The industry you find yourself in has a way of playing games with your mind, and this can get you angry. Entrepreneurs in the financial niche experience this a lot. One day the market is bullish, the next day it is so bearish that their portfolio is greatly affected. They would then sell off their assets to cut their losses, and immediately they do, the market becomes bullish. This is just an example with financial markets like the stock and cryptocurrency industry. Every industry has its peculiarities that can leave entrepreneurs angry.

- **Your employees/team.** Human beings are difficult to control. Your team comprises different individuals with different backgrounds, ideologies, experiences, skills, goals, and so on. It is a huge task to streamline these diversities in one direction. In your quest to do this, a member(s) of your team would still want to deviate from the cause. This can be upsetting.

- **Your competition.** Your competition is always out to get on your nerves. Everything they do is a subtle message informing you that you are in a war with them. An instance that readily comes to mind is the

122

Coca-Cola vs. Pepsi Cola war, in which the two companies always take a jibe at each other with their ads. For example, there is this Pepsi commercial where a little boy buys two cans of Coke, only to step on them for height to reach for the button to get a can of Pepsi. In another ad, a Coke truck driver tastes Pepsi for the first time and refuses to share the drink with anyone else. These are just a few examples where the Cola Wars have gotten messy. Coca-Cola is not exonerated; they have thrown their fair share of blows, though mostly as a response to Pepsi's commercial. The bottom line is this: Your competition can get you angry through different forms. They would try to elicit a negative response from you. Do not give in to their antics.

-   **Yourself.** There are times when you'd get angry at yourself. You'd get angry at the mistakes you made. You'd get angry at failing at a venture. You'd get angry for missing a business opportunity. You'd get angry for employing the wrong hand. You'd get angry for purchasing the wrong equipment. You'd get angry for not starting early. Sometimes, your anger would morph into sadness. At other times, frustration. And at other times, recklessness because you are trying to meet up with what you think you've lost.

No matter the reason for your anger, never let the anger control you. Remember, *the angry general* (read: entrepreneur) *would be provoked into taking superficial action.* Superficial action here means an action or decision without depth, without a solid foundation. An action that is bound to crumble and probably take the business down with it. So, choose to respond to the anger positively. Use anger as a raw material to build a solid business. Neil Patel, a former contributor for Forbes, outlines different ways to use anger as a raw material to build a solid business.[19] I will use Patel's ideas as solutions to handle the five areas of your life and business that can get you angry.

-   *What do you do when you are angry at life?*

Neil suggested that you should **be more perseverant**. These were his words: "I know I've felt deflated and defeated on more than a few occasions because things simply weren't going my way. However, I've found that anger is perhaps the best emotion for pumping me back up and giving it another go." This means that you should channel your anger into demanding what you want from life. Get angry with the state of things and determine to change them. Let anger be your spur to have a better life, a better business.

-   *What do you do when you are angry at your market/ industry?*

Still persevere. Remember that the market moves in trends and cycles. What goes up would surely come down. The market is a sinuous wave of highs and lows. In your anger, persevere, be patient. You will surely win.

In addition to being more perseverant, use your anger to **eliminate fear**. You get angry at the market because you fear you are going to lose your investment.

It is a chain: fear births anger, anger births desperation, and desperation births carelessness. Neil stated that anger helps slash through his anxieties. It helps him take action instead of focusing on the hypotheticals.

According to him, it is scientifically proven. Citing *Psychology Today*, he wrote, Anger causes levels of the stress hormone cortisol to drop, suggesting that anger helps people calm down and get ready to address a problem -- not run from it.

- *What do you when you are angry at your employees/ team?*

Your anger can be effective in two ways. First, use it to **improve communication** with the team. Sometimes, we need anger to express how we truly feel about a bad situation. Some people get angry yet find it difficult to express themselves because they do not want to hurt the offender. But this shouldn't be so. Neil pointed out that letting the anger come through would help you communicate how you are feeling. He added that "Getting a little pissed now and then allows you to cut through the BS and tell it like it really is."

Also, your anger can **aid in negotiation**. Remember, we are talking about your employees *or team*. Members of your team include your investors, partners, and other people or organizations tied to your business one way or another. So if you, according to Neil, find yourself "getting the short end of the stick, getting a little pissed is sometimes all you need to put your foot down and negotiate like a boss. This ensures that you're nobody's doormat and gives you the courage to do whatever it takes to get your needs met."

- *What do you do when you are angry at your competition?*

The answer is simple: When they go low, go high. Be the one to get them angry by not responding the way they want you to. **Show your humanness** in all its entirety. Being angry is a part of being human, but after getting angry, be the bigger person.

Do not try to pull the competition down even though they are trying to play a dirty game. The world is watching, and the customers know who is offering real value. Don't allow the competition to get you into taking superficial decisions that would only hurt you and your business in the end.

- *What do you do when you are angry at yourself?*

This is where the bulk of the work lies. Everything about your business may not continue and end with you, but it will definitely start with you. And the beginning of a venture is important for its sustainability and success. There are five things you can do when you are angry with yourself.

First, you can **achieve hyper-focus**. At that point of anger, kill the emotion and birth the feeling. Anger comes with muddled thoughts. That is one of the physiological responses it produces. But you can counter this with your feelings. Choose calmness. Neil wrote that when he's angry, he becomes obsessed with the source of his irritation. But he overcomes this and all the obsession melts away. He becomes "like a horse with blinders dead set on accomplishing whatever goal is at hand." Use your anger to gain clarity of purpose, to be more focused on your goals.

Second, use your anger to **boost your confidence**. Recall that fear births anger. Just like anger can be used to conquer fear, it can also be used simultaneously to boost confidence. Quoting Evans and Foster, Neil wrote: "Get mad and the automatic rush of adrenaline heightens your senses and reduces your inhibitions."

After this, you can now **ignite your passion**. Fear can take away your zeal towards your goal, and one veritable way of getting your passion is through anger. Use your anger to (re)ignite your passion. Neil pointed out that "it's hard to only be lukewarm about something when you're in a fit of rage," but using anger intelligently helps you approach a task or a goal with zest and zeal, which would ultimately lead to great results. It also gives you the assurance that you can take on any challenge and leads you to the fourth thing to do: **take action**.

Let your anger be your spur. This time let your anger not make you punch the wall or throw away a flower vase. Take bold steps towards getting what you want for yourself and your business. On taking action, Neil had this to say of himself: "For me personally, a little bit of good anger makes me feel like I'm ready to take on the world. If I was only half-invested in a project beforehand, getting angry can be the catalyst for me actually getting it done."

Then, after all these, let your anger **provide self-insight**. Neil said he uses anger as a means of personal reflection to shine a light on his imperfections, and it has helped him grow and progress. Like Neil, use anger to analyze your situation. Understand why you got angry in the first place. What went wrong? Was the fault from you? How can you make things better? How do you ensure that there is not a repeat of whatever went wrong? Anger is a good motivation for going back to the drawing board.

❖ Self-conceit

"Self-conceited generals are easy to shame." - Sun Vu

Sun Vu's quote above summarizes the danger of self-conceit. Undue arrogance does not pay. In this era, many confuse self-conceit with self-confidence. They are not the same. Self-conceit is simply arrogance. Merriam-Webster Dictionary defines it as an *"exaggerated* opinion of one's own qualities or abilities."[20] Same dictionary defines self-confidence as "confidence in oneself and in one's powers and abilities." [21] And the word "confidence" means "a feeling or consciousness of one's powers or of reliance on one's circumstances."[22] Notice that these words have similar meanings, but what separates self-conceit from self-confidence is the operative word, "exaggerated."

It is good to be confident of your abilities and qualities. This is why we have egos—to give us the sense of worth we deserve. But when this confidence becomes exaggerated, then we are crossing a very dangerous line. Do not overestimate your worth to the point of dampening the worth of another. There is a difference between saying, "We are the best online school in Europe," and "We are the best online school in Europe, unlike ABC school and XYZ academy, which do not have the capacity we have." The former is you having an opinion about your ability and quality (confidence), while the latter exaggerates that ability and quality by pulling down the ability and quality of others (self-conceit).

Sun Vu rightly pointed out that the arrogant or self-conceited general (or, in this case, entrepreneur) is easy to shame. This was the case of one of the favorite examples in this book—Blackberry.

The Economic Times stated one of the reasons for Blackberry's fall was "institutional arrogance."[23] Institutional arrogance is "offensive and incorrect certainty of correctness by an entity or person with artificial power within a narrow space of influence."[24] Mike Lazaridis and Jim Balsillie, The CEOs of RIM, makers of Blackberry, felt that Apple and Google's innovation couldn't bring down Blackberry. "Balsillie and Lazaridis believed it was far too soon to seriously entertain the idea of putting a computer on a phone, and Apple and Google were able to outmaneuver them through simple technological superiority."[25] Simply put: Apple and Google easily shamed Blackberry.

❖ **People pleasing**

"General who loves the people easily gets troubled." - Sun Vu

Know this: You cannot please everyone, no matter how hard you try. This is one of the major reasons many have failed in business. Some entrepreneurs want to be tagged, "The (wo)man of the people," so they go out of their way trying to please everyone—from investors to employees to clients. What hurts about being a people pleaser is that most times, the people you are trying to please do not really care about you or your business. They just want you as a medium to meet their desires. And once that is granted, they move on.

Being a people pleaser is never rewarding. Like Sun Vu pointed out, it only leaves you troubled. You end up giving up what is best for your business because you are considering what is good for everyone. Your product or service cannot satisfy everyone. This is why you have competition. Healthy competition is good for the market or industry because, one way or another, each company is meeting the specific needs of the clients in the market. You have your target market; those who love and value your product. Those are the people you should be concerned about.

Also, when you are out to please people all the time, you end up burning yourself out. Your mind becomes a rowdy marketplace filled with thoughts of how to satisfy everyone's needs at the same time. This would tell on your mental and physical health. And the truth is: you cannot keep up with this behavior. Therefore, the best thing to do is to stop it completely. Investors, employees, and clients will have more regard for you when they know that you are kind yet firm, empathetic yet uncompromising, especially when it comes to your business. Being a smart species, humans can perceive when you are always out to please them, and since they love the attention, they will milk the opportunity and take you for granted.

So, don't get yourself into trouble. Do not sacrifice your personal values or that of your company on the altar of wanting to be the good (wo)man to and for everyone. You cannot do that. No one can.

Act right in times of uncertainty and also avoid the five drawbacks at all cost. These drawbacks are dangerous because they deal directly with you. It is easier to rectify drawbacks that stem from other factors like your staff, investors, or competitors, but one drawback from you could destroy everything you've built in a flash. You are the foundation of the vision. You have to protect yourself. Your business, and everything attached to it, needs you to function optimally.

Pledge to Action

I affirm that:

I will make room for contingencies.

I understand that they are part of life.

I understand that I am a terrain, so I avow to be a favorable one so that I can station my forces.

I will not linger on a barren land.

I will think straight at all times.

I will not cross the roads of impatience and non-delegation.

My competitors can sometimes be my collaborators and partners.

I am prepared to work with them if it is necessary.

I will not be reckless with myself or my company.

I let go of greed.

I let go of anger.

I will not puncture the ego of others to inflate mine.

I am confident in my abilities.

I am committed to treating my employees and customers with respect.

I will not be a people-pleaser.

I understand my worth.

I will not make mistakes at times of uncertainty and despair.

I know how to handle contingencies.

CHAPTER NINE

The Resilience

"Resilience is accepting your new reality, even if it's less good than the one you had before. You can fight it, you can do nothing but scream about what you've lost, or you can accept that and try to put together something that's good."

— Elizabeth Edwards

Entrepreneurs are the lifeblood of commerce and the cutthroat world of business. The business realm is fiercely competitive all over the world. Therefore, business owners should arm themselves with everything that brings about positive business ideals. One of such ideals is resilience.

Markets are bound to experience downturns. Think of the Asia financial crash of 1997. The dotcom bubble of 2000. The economic meltdown of 2008. And the Covid-19 crash of 2020. Businesses that will win in the long run are those that are resilient enough to withstand harsh market conditions. As an entrepreneur, you should learn to come up with decisive actions that would boost business resilience.

Business resilience is the positive ability of a company to adapt to the consequences of catastrophe. It is like the adversity quotient for businesses. Other factors embedded in business resilience include crisis management, business continuity, risk assessments and management, and the ability of an organization to adapt, thrive, and survive in a new environment.

Resilience strategies are crucial to businesses because unless they are in place, most businesses would not be able to thrive or recover from unexpected changes or disruptions in the market. Business survival and ultimate business success are tied to business resilience. According to Eleanor Murray, a senior fellow in management practices at the University of Oxford Saïd Business School, the creation of resilience is an iterative learning process.[1] It is continuous. It is a trait that should be consciously and continuously developed.

This means rather than trying to bounce back to where the business was, you cultivate new ways to take it forward. For instance, according to Murray, businesses learn from previous disruptions and incorporate the learning process into their businesses as they move forward.[2] Most business schools focus on the financial growth of a business, which isn't particularly surprising, considering that financial performance, is perhaps the most famous metric used to gauge business success. The repercussion, however, is that most entrepreneurs do not prepare adequate resilient strategies for the future.

To spearhead a thriving and flourishing business in times of uncertainty is one of the most daunting tasks entrepreneurs face. Our world today is highly dynamic and unpredictable. Business systems are constantly being stretched to breaking point. This is why it is necessary to create new fundamental approaches and models for businesses. And these approaches must incorporate interdependence, systems thinking, and new perspectives.

Resilience must analyze risks that are not easily seen or prepared for, and it must consider the changes in the immediate environment of the business, and how they can be used as an advantage for the business. It requires new levels to critical thinking, and the ability to conduct proper analysis beneath the surface of things.

The *Harvard Business Review* outlined six principles by which businesses can develop resilience.

One: The business must learn the art of adaptation. Adapting means learning to survive in spite of circumstances. It requires some level of diversity, and it can be attained through natural or planned experimentation. Adaptive processes and structures are established so that businesses can learn how to be flexible and diversify.

Two: The business should have diverse ways of responding to new disruptions or stress levels in the business environment. The advantage of this is that all systems that propel the business do not fail or collapse. Diversity also involves hiring different people from different backgrounds who have distinctive skills and cognitive abilities. It creates new ways of thinking and new methods of doing things.

Three: Redundancy is yet another resilient structure. It is a sort of protection against uncertainty. It is created by duplicating elements (for example, having many factories that produce the same product) or by having different elements (both human and non-human resources) working towards the same goal.

Four: A modular system allows certain aspects of the business to fail without the whole system falling and collapsing. If the business can be divided into smaller parts, then it is more understandable and can be recalibrated during a time of crisis.

Five: Prudence is another resilience strategy. It operates on the principle of caution and creates scenarios of possible situations that have incredible consequences on the fate of a business. Contingency plans, working out scenarios, monitoring signals early, and constant analysis of the business systems are ways to institute prudence in business resilience goals.

Six: The business must align its goals and activities with broader systems. Business corporations are positioned within several elements —from supply chains to business ecosystems, economies, etc. Therefore to develop resilience, businesses need to have clearly defined purposes for contributing effectively to society. When a business venture is a friend to society, it is unlikely that it will have any disruptions, and even if it does, it can easily be propelled back to the top. For instance, Google, Apple, Amazon, Tesla and Netflix are businesses that are positively interwoven into society.

Another key way of building business resilience is to intermix the business portfolio. It also involves taking risks that are educated and calculated. It involves the ability to spot opportunities from afar. Having a diverse portfolio helps a business from falling in times of adversity.

Also, collaboration and cooperation are veritable ways by which business resilience can increase. Through collective resilience, businesses can have shared assets that provide insurance through investments.

They can also access new capabilities, new skills, and professionalism. Powerful alliances have always proven to be prime assets in the long run, for ages. Remember competitive collaboration.

But before resilience can be built into a business, one important factor must come into play first—and this, your resilience.

The Role of Leadership in Resilience

A business can only be resilient if you are resilient. You are the powerhouse of the business both in good and bad times. To maintain business resilience in times of adversity, you need to learn how to act, adapt, and anticipate.

You need to be at the top of your game. You need to be informed about everything that can affect your business. This is where qualitative knowledge, quantitative knowledge, and knowledge of causal relationships come into play. You need to ask key questions like: How can we tackle upcoming challenges? What strategies are in place for the survival of the business? How can we turn a challenge into an advantage? These questions need to be critically analyzed if you are to make informed decisions.

You must learn how to think quickly on your feet and act with decisive action if you want to adapt fast to new business climates. New strategies would have to emerge in all spheres—from branding to employee performance to team building.

It is also your responsibility to diversify business networks and create opportunities for other capabilities and skills to thrive. The world has transcended into the era of digital communication, so people with the right skills in that field should be brought on board to work if your business still slacks in that area.

Business resilience can be developed from three key areas. I have termed these areas the pillars of resilience. They are Vision, Productivity, and Assets and Liabilities.

The Pillars of Resilience

1. **Vision:** The number one pillar of business resilience is Vision. Everything else written above would be highly impossible if they aren't envisioned in the first place. The resilience of your vision translates into the resilience of your business so as you develop your vision, you must ensure that such vision is strong enough to withstand forthcoming challenges. Ask yourself these questions:

    - Am I tenacious?

    - Does my vision align with my tenacity?

    - Can my vision thrive in every environment?

    - What are my ambitions? Are they well laid out?

    - Is there a consistent drive to accomplish them?

2. **Productivity:** A resilient leader will build a resilient team, and together they will build a resilient business. You need to review employee productivity and teamwork from time to time.

    - Do the employees share the same goals and vision?

    - How much fire and dedication do they have towards the growth of the business?

    - Are they ready to work tirelessly and relentlessly to build business resilience in uncertainty?

3. **Assets and Liabilities:** The ability to have invaluable assets that can see a business through thick and thin is perhaps the most intricate part of business intelligence.

    - How diversified is the business?

    - What kind of assets or network does it have as a sustainable strategy?

The survival of a business depends solely on how much work has been put into making it resilient over time. The only way your business can flourish and blossom is when you think about it in a futuristic sense.

Pledge to Action

I affirm that:

I am a resilient entrepreneur.

I will build my business to be resilient.

My business will withstand every storm that comes in the market.

I am strong.

My team is tenacious.

We are productive.

Together, we will build a resilient company.

CHAPTER TEN

Using Spies

"You can only get ahead of your competition when you know things they don't know and do things they don't do."

— Ma Trong Tham

Spies are important in battle. They offer intelligence to the general. They inform the general about the enemy's plans, weapons, strategies, strengths, weaknesses—everything. Spies are valuable to the general but detrimental to the enemy.

In business, it is necessary you use spies. There are information or perspectives you cannot access unless you have certain people around you who offer this information. Your goal is to win as an entrepreneur, and you need all the information you can get to stay ahead in the game.

Now, spying in business is not new. In fact, it goes by different names— "corporate espionage," "industrial espionage," "economic espionage," or "corporate spying." The activities under corporate espionage or spying include trespassing a competitor's property, accessing files without a competitor's permission, posing as a competitor's employee in order to learn confidential information like trade secrets, hacking a competitor's computers, wiretapping a competitor, or instigating a malware attack on a competitor's website.[1]

These are all criminal activities backed by desperation and malicious intent. I would *never* recommend that. However, Josh Fruhlinger noted that there is form of corporate spying that is not illegal (at least according to the companies that practice it). This form of spying is called "competitive intelligence." It involves gathering and analyzing information that is mostly public but that has the capacity to affect competitor's fortunes such as mergers, acquisitions, new government regulations, and so on.

For instance, a company may research an executive in a rival company to try to understand the executive's motivations and behavior, and use this information to predict the next action of the company.[2] This may sound simple, harmless, and legal, but I would not recommend it either for a reason: you may not know when you cross the divide between legal and illegal.

So the question is: If I don't recommend corporate spying because it is illegal, and I also do not recommend competitive intelligence because it may become illegal, what then do I recommend?

I have developed a concept of spying on your competitors without actually spying on them. My method will allow you to get information about a rival company without even getting to know their trade secrets or any confidential information. If used effectively, my method will also give you access to information your competitor *may* not know about. This method is nothing elaborate. It is a simple means of obtaining intelligence you may even have thought about. I have termed it "The Strategy of Indirect Spying."

Before I go into this method, I need to state a fundamental point: Legal or true spying or espionage should only try to gain information about the products in the market or the market itself. Once spying or espionage crosses the line of obtaining confidential information about the competition, then it becomes a problem.

The Strategy of Indirect Spying shows you two ways you can obtain information about the products in the market or the market itself. The information gotten through this strategy can put you miles ahead of the competition.

The first method is to **become a customer**. Get into the market and blend in like a customer. You can do this or members of your team could do it for you. Interact with other customers and middlemen in the market. By doing this, you would get undiluted information about the strengths and weaknesses of not just the competition's product, but your product as well.

Before a customer commends or lays a complaint to a company, that customer has most likely aired their opinion to more than two end users. The customer may not register their commendation or complaint exhaustively when they reach out to customer care due to the formal atmosphere around such conversations. Customers or end users bare their heart in the marketplace—among other end users.

So, get into the marketplace. Be active on social media. Listen to what is said about your product or your industry. Engage social listening: monitor social media channels for mentions of your brand, competitors, products, and so on.[3] Tony Tran noted that social listening differs from social monitoring. In social monitoring, you track metrics like brand mentions, relevant hashtags, competitor mentions, and industry trends. Social listening is much deeper—you track the mood or sentiment behind these metrics.[4] And it is this information that can distinguish you from your competitors. This is why Warren Buffet got the name the Oracle of Omaha. He didn't just use numbers to predict price movements of stock, he understood the emotions, sentiments, and psychology of the market.

With social listening, you can get information about your competitor without using corporate espionage or competitive intelligence. Tony Tran wrote: "Social listening is more than understanding what people say about you. You also want to know what they say about your competitors. This gives you important insights into where you fit in the marketplace. You will also learn what your competitors are up to in real-time. Are they launching new products? Developing new marketing campaigns? Taking a beating in the press? Social listening allows you to find out about these new opportunities and threats as they happen, so you can plan and respond accordingly."[5]

So why go through the negative route when there is a positive one? This means that the Road of Corporate Espionage is another route you shouldn't follow, especially in moments of crisis when you may be forced to take *desperate* actions.

While you are in the market as a customer and engaging in social listening, you can proceed with the second method of the strategy of indirect spying.

Be part of a premium community. Not every information about your industry or market is available on social media or on Google. You have to be part of a *premium* and *exclusive* community to gain access to such information. This is a lesson you can pick from investors or traders in financial markets like the stock market, cryptocurrency market, etc. Advanced investors or traders often belong to communities where they get information about a company or the industry before such information is made public. This is why they buy assets at low prices and sell at high prices when the information has hit the market and driven up the asset's value. This is why they also sell out assets early when they get news of a possible market crash.

As an entrepreneur, you cannot underestimate the importance of belonging to a premium and exclusive community if you want to be on top of the food chain.

You can only get ahead of your competition when you know things they don't know and do things they don't do. A veritable way to do this is by spying—a different kind of spying.

Pledge to Action

I affirm that:

I want to win at all times.

But I wouldn't take any illegal route to win.

I will win by hard work.

I will win by getting access to the right information.

I will win by empathy, by understanding the customer needs.

I will win by joining the right community.

I will win by using the right spies.

CONCLUSION

Entrepreneurship is a fierce battleground. The battle never stops. You would always be in a constant battle with yourself—trying to be better than who you were yesterday. You would be in a constant battle with your team—trying to get them to align with the vision. You would be in a constant battle with your competition—trying to outpace them.

Warfare is never easy. But some armies and generals have a record of never losing a battle. Sun Vu was one of them. And I have replicated his strategies for you to use in your business. I believe the ideas in this book are all you need to be on a constant victory march as an entrepreneur.

Because you have read this book, I know you are not afraid of entrepreneurship's many battles. I know you have the assurance that you are on a pathway to victory. Bask in this assurance always. I hope to see you at the top soon.

Author Compliment

THE LAW OF WAR

兵法

The Art Of Competition Benefits In

War, Business, And Life

Sun Vu

孫 武

Translated by

Ma Trong Tham

A Few Words

The Law of War is one of the old Chinese writings that have been around as far back as the 5th century BC. This book is composed of thirteen chapters, and it is said to have been composed by the popular war strategist of that time named Sun Vu (who, of course, is now globally known as Sun Tzu – the author of the equally popular treatise called The Art of War). In a way, it seems like Sun and his work suffered a change in name over times. While his original name was Sun Vu, he became popular with Sun Tzu. Similarly, his work The Law of War, after many years, became The Art of War.

Each chapter of this book (The Law of War) focuses on a particular situation of warfare and its relation to the strategy and tactics inherent in military affairs, especially ones that deal with battle of every aspect – either land or water. The lessons therein have been adopted by various war generals for hundreds of years, and it is still a relevant work even today, as I have no doubt it will continue to be for hundreds of more years to come. For about 1,500 years, The Law of War, has remained the leading work in a collection of ancient works that became formalized as the by Emperor Shenzong of Song in 1080. He listed The Law of War as one of the Seven Military Classics of ancient times. This incredible work has maintained the reputation of not only being the most influential text about strategy in warfare in East Asia, but has also influenced the lifestyle, legal strategy, business tactics and military organization in both the East and the West.

Arguably, no other book about the analysis of the Chinese military is as detailed as The Law of War. It touches on very important areas as the use of weapons, the application of strategy during battle, and the process of discipline. It also highlights how necessary it is to make use of intelligent operatives and espionage to increase the chance of success during battle and every other aspect of warfare. Indeed, it is safe to say that most of the modern military cultures of today have their origin from The Law of War. This is why the lessons taught in this book will continue to be relevant for many generations to come; it has formed the basis of military trainings of today all over the world and it shall continue to be for more thousands of years.

While this particular book has been translated into various languages, including Vietnamese, it was partially translated to English by British officer Everard Ferguson Calthrop in the early 20th century; and it came with the title The Book of War, but the translation was completed five years later by Lionel Giles.

Many have drawn inspiration from the lessons in The Law of War; some of these people include political and military leaders all over the world – American military general Norman Schwarzkopf Jr., Vietnamese general Ngô Quang Trưởng, Japanese daimyō Takeda Shingen, amongst a lot of other powerful people of the world.

Cao Cao, the poet, warlord and strategist wrote the earliest known commentary about Sun Vu's work during the early 3rd century AD; his writing was reportedly the earliest known commentary about the book. Cao Cao himself admitted in his preface that he removed certain passages from the original, and he also changed many words. So it was not really clear how much of a change he made to the original work. Also, in the early 20th century, about the time the work was being translated to English by Calthrop and Giles, the Chinese writer and reformer Liang Qichao explained that the texts of The Law of War were actually written in the 4th century BC by the descendant of Sun Vu – the name of this descendant was Sun Bin.

Over the years, the thirteen chapters contained in the work have also suffered a change in titles. For chapter 1, it was titled Laying Plans by Lionel Giles in 1910, The Calculations by R.L. Wing in 1988, and Initial Estimation by Ralph D. Sawyer in 1996. Different changes also occurred in the subsequent thirteen chapters. This book, also, has peculiar titles for each of the thirteen chapters it contains. Planning, Combating, Offensive Strategy, Military Disposition, Military Force, Real and Unreal, Maneuvering, Nine Changes, Marching, Terrain, Nine Ground Positions, Fire Attack, and Using Spy.

The first illustrates all that is required to understand the nature of war, and planning for the war is one of the most important elements of the tactics and strategy of warfare. The second chapter directly goes into the art of combating enemy during battle; it explains the entire angles one must consider before deciding to engage enemy in combat. Sometimes, combat can be more of psychological than physical. The third chapter introduces the strategy of taking enemy by surprise and showing that one has broader strategy than the enemy. Chapter four observes the method of making the enemy troop miserable by doing everything possible to take the comfort off of them and rendering them totally powerless. Chapter five explains the principles that guide the control of military forces, either a large force or a small one. It shows that the same principle guides whatever number the force might be. Chapter six stresses the benefit of arriving early at the battle ground, especially before the enemy troop – it shows the advantage of being the first troop to occupy the ground. The seventh chapter is all about maneuvering against the enemy by making proper use of the soldiers. In most cases, it is better to improvise, depending on the situation of the war. The eighth chapter highlights all the changes that may affect the result of a war. Some of these changes could be the road, the weather, the weapons, or even the soldiers. Chapter nine explains the process of moving soldiers to the battlefield, and surviving the rigors of the terrains. Chapter ten further assesses the terrains of war; it observes all the grounds and points, then how to bear responsibility as a war general. Chapter eleven introduces the nine ground positions and how to manage each of them, depending on the nature of the war and the application of military power. The twelfth chapter teaches how to make use of fire to attack the enemy; it explains the five ways one can make use of the fire to decimate the enemy and render the troop powerless. And lastly, the thirteenth chapter emphasizes the importance of making use of spies during war. It does not only talk about the use of one's spies but also discovering enemy spies and making use of them to one's advantage. All these thirteen chapters are necessary for a war general who aspires to emerge victorious during war.

The Law of War is not only applicable to military strategy alone, it is also applicable to life. For in a way, life itself is like a warfront, and one must be ready to fight the battles it brings and come out victorious in the end. Life comes with many challenges, and only a man armed with the necessary knowledge of war and knows the right application of tactics would not be defeated.

In East Asia, The Law of War has become a part of the syllabus for candidates of military service examinations. Takeda Shingen was invincible in battle because he read the works of Sun Vu which gave him great inspiration against the battle of Fūrinkazan. Some South Vietnamese officers during the Vietnam War extensively studied The Law of War so much that they could recite every passage of the book from their heads.

Generally, The Law of War teaches how to outsmart one's opponent without having to engage in physical combat or battle, as the case may be.

About Sun Vu

Sun Vu, popularly known as Sun Tzu, was born in 545 BC and died in 470 BC; he was 75 years old – this was during the period known as 'The Spring and Autumn Period of China'. Vu, who is also believed to have authored the globally acclaimed book The Art of War, was a military expert, a general and a philosopher. His book is one of the best books that deal with strategies and theories of the warfare. Only few people in the West may know that his original name is Sun Vu, and that the Tzu only means 'Master', which, of course, is a title of respect, especially in ancient Chinese.

A lot of details about Sun Vu are sketchy, and most of what we know today comes from Ssu-ma Ch'ien's Shi Chi. According to the Grand Historian records, Sun Vu was born in the State of Qi. But there was further controversy about his birth; the Spring and Autumn Annals of Wu and Yueh maintained that he was born in Wu. It is hard to really determine Sun Wu's true origin since it's a very long time ago that he existed; records are sometimes bound to contradict themselves.

Even details about Sun Vu's early life are blurry. All that is known is that Vu grew up in a military family and he studied military science. The only fact that stands out is that Sun Vu, at some point in his life, became a great strategist and general in the military. In fact, he was a general for King Helü of Wu where it was recorded that he won many wars, especially the ones most people already thought he would lose. With hi strategic thinking and brilliant maneuvering, he was able to conquer a lot of enemies.

Sun won his battles in various unique manners. Most times, he would win without actually fighting his enemies. He was known to always analyze battles and decide whether it was necessary to fight or not. Instead of picking up arms and charging head-on toward his enemies, Sun Vu would rather make use of spies to discover the chink in the enemies' armors. Sun Vu was one of the earliest generals to make use of spies. And whenever it was necessary for him to fight, he would also attack in manners the enemies never saw coming because he understood warfare strategies better than a lot of his opponents. And when the battle was over, he would not only win but also have the least number of casualties – he rarely lost his men.

Also according to historical reports, Sun Vu was believed to be the victor during the Battle of Boju in 506 BC. Sima Qian (145/135 – 86 BC), who authored the Shiji regarded Sun Vu as an outstanding strategist; he explained that Vu was not only a flexible commanded but also had an unlimited surprises for his enemies. His opponents were always quaking in their boots whenever they discovered that Sun Vu was the opposing general, for they never knew what Sun Vu's point of attack would be, or method as the case would be. In almost 40 years as a general, Vu never lost a war or battle – he kept a clean sheet all through his life.

The Art of War, written by Sun Tzu, was originally titled The Law of War; but for some reasons The Law of War became The Art of War in the West. This book was one of the earliest books that explained the concept of warfare. As one of the most influential books ever, it has been read by kings and commanders for over two thousand years; and it has successfully influenced a lot of battles historically. According to an historical report, it was written on bamboo slats that were joined together by a twine; it became a widely popular book even in the western world, and it wasn't translated into English until the 20th century.

In the times of Sun Vu, war was seen as a form of chivalry, and it was considered the sport of rich people of noble backgrounds. But Vu refused to see any nobility, chivalry or sport in war. To him, war was a brutal battle between two opposing forces that ultimately leads to deaths and destruction – and if you want to play the game, you should as well know how to play it right; hence his decision to write the book. So Sun Vu used the Taoist principles to further his warfare strategies;

and in no time he became a force to reckon with in the battle field. By merging the principles with war strategies, Sun Vu succeeded in changing the rules of war - which, of course, were conventional at the time. He came up with sure methods that won him a lot of battles.

Many historians agreed that Sun Vu's mind worked differently from others in his rank. Unlike other generals who fancied long campaigns and the systematic dance around the bush, Vu knew that war was a serious business which should not be handled with levity. You must strike when the iron is hot, and you must strike very hard. It is the first blow that will determine how the fight will end. He believed that as soon as war started, the ultimate goal was to defeat the enemy. With this knowledge, Sun Vu knew that he must not follow the conventional method of warfare; he must carve out his own path, create his own niche. He didn't follow the basic wisdom that ruled the art of war in his time. So when it was time for battle, the other generals were always simply unprepared for Sun Vu's tactics.

Because of him, basic military concepts were changed and improved for thousands of years. Even in the Gulf War, American generals Norman Schwarzkopf, Jr and Colin Powell applied the principles inherent in The Art of War.

Today, Sun Vu's name remains on the tongues of most army generals of the world.

Chapter 1 – Planning[1] 始計

Understanding the nature of war is a nationally important task. War is the point where life and death meet. It is the path to destruction or survival. So war must be scrutinized. War has five determinants that we must plan. We must understand their correlations. One is righteousness.[2] Two is atmosphere. Three is terrain. Four is the general. Five is martial law.

Righteousness is a way of making people willing to join with the king, to make them unite and join forces, to live and die with courage. Atmosphere is the night or day, hotness or coldness, and change of four seasons. Terrain is high or low ground, near or far distance, easy or difficult roads, plains or canyons and the conditions of survival. The general must be strategic, trustworthy, kind, courageous and strict. Martial law means the organization, management of soldiers and expenditures in the military.

The general must know all the five determinants explained above because if he knows, he will win and if he doesn't know, he will lose. So he has to calculate carefully in planning and find out their actual correlations. Therefore, the general must compare the following seven situations:

1. Which party has the righteous king?

2. Which party has the talented general?

3. Which party benefits more from the atmosphere and terrain?

4. Which party abides by martial law?

5. Which party owns the better more sophisticated weapons?

6. Which party's soldiers train more frequently?

7. Which party rewards and punishes more fairly?

Based on the answers to these questions, we know which party will win and which party will fail.

We should keep the generals who obey the instructions given above because they will win. We should get rid of the generals who do not obey the instructions given above because they will fail.

When planning for advantage according to the advice above, act on the situation and take advantage of factors outside that common rule. To act according to the situation is to take advantage by adjusting the plan that flexibly, improvably[3], and firmly grasps the initiatives.

War tactics should follow the principle of deception. So when one has the power, appear powerless.   When one deploys, appear not use soldiers. When one wants to fight near, seem to want to fight faraway. When one wants to get close, seem to be backing away. When enemy tries to find an advantage then one uses small benefits to lure them. When enemy disorders, one advances. If the enemy is strong enough, one can guard against them. If the enemy is lithe and strong then one will temporarily avoid them. If the enemy is aggressive, one harasses. If enemy is guarded and cautious, one makes them arrogant. If the enemy is rested, one disturbs them. If enemy is united, one wants to divide them. If the enemy does not defend, one will surprisingly attack them. Attack where enemy is not prepared, appears where enemy least expects. So we can see that in war, surprise is the key to victory.

Those are the basic strategies of the generals to harvest successfully. It must be flexible but improvised, not guided or anticipated.

Before fighting, the right calculation[4] and proper planning[5] will result in victory, whereas incomplete planning before the battle will not bring victory.   So to ensure complete victory, complete planning is the condition that must be met. If the plan is sketchy and there are only few winning conditions, such a plan is bound to end in failure. So based on this analysis, it will be easy to determine who will win and who will be defeated.

Chapter 2 – Combating 作戰

During combat, we usually mobilize an army[1] of one thousand light chariots[2], one thousand heavy chariots[3], and hundred thousand armored soldiers[4]. Food must travel thousands of "li"[5] along with forward and backward costs. The reception of guests, expenses such as materials for making weapons, repairing chariots, weapons, etc. cost thousands of taels[6] of gold every day. All these must be ready before marching a hundred thousand soldiers to the battlefield.

With such an army in the battlefield, quick victory must be achieved. Being on the battlefield for too long is not ideal. Delay in combat will make the weapons rust and soldiers will begin to lose their morale; and if the enemy discovers this weakness, an attack will be inevitable. There is no better moment to attack than when the enemy is weary and seems hopeless.

Although I have heard about reckless combat, I have never seen a delay in combat that is considered wise. Using soldiers to fight a battle for an unnecessarily long time is really unprecedented. Only someone who understands the danger that comes from such a careless strategy will understand the resulting effect.

A person who is good at using soldiers does not recruit soldiers twice and does not transport food three times. A good general uses domestic weapons but uses the enemy's food to feed the troops, so the soldiers are well fed.

When the military has to travel a very long distance to fight the battle, the national treasury is often left empty and the citizens suffer the effect. It is highly expensive to maintain the financial cost of war. Close to the garrison, the price is expensive. Whenever prices go up, the national treasure runs the risk of running out; and if the treasure is exhausted, taxes will have to be raised to keep up. Hundred of the citizens suffer this for when the tax is raised, a lot of them run out of money. The longer the soldiers stay on the battlefield, the more it costs the people. Yet, there is no certainty of victory. The weary soldiers are decreasing on the battle front and the people remain poor at home. An average wealth of ten is depleted to seven. More expenses on the battlefield such as damaged chariots, lame horses, additional weapons, armor, large buffalo, heavy chariots, etc of ten are depleted by six.

Those are the reasons why a wise general always forages food from enemy. Eating one "bushel"[8] of enemy's food will save us the rigor of bringing along twenty. Using one "picul"[9] of haulm and grass will help us to cut twenty picul of haulm and grass to raise horses.

For our soldiers, anger must be the impetus to destroy the enemy and the reward must be the stimulus to defeat the enemy. If one wants brave army to fight, one must encourage morale. If one wants soldiers to forage enemy food, one must reward them. Therefore, in the chariots battle, out of ten or more chariots won, the soldiers who won the first chariot were rewarded. After that, we added our flag and then mixed into our army. We treated the surrendered soldiers well and used them. By convincing the surrendered army to join us, we have strategically increased our strength.

Therefore, we see that in combat only the quick victory matters and there is no reward for extending a campaign. A general who truly understands warfare controls the fate of the people and is a master of national security.

Chapter 3 – Offensive Strategy 謀攻

In military maneuvering, the supreme art of war is to keep our nation intact as a superior policy; taking over an undamaged enemy nation is more appropriately than breaking it. Keeping our army[1] whole is the best policy, capturing all the enemy troops is better than killing them. Keeping an entire brigade[2] of our own is superior, capturing an entire brigade of the enemy is better than breaking them. Keeping an entire regiment[3] of our own is superior, capturing an entire regiment of the enemy is better than breaking them. Keeping an entire battalion[4] of our own is superior, capturing an entire battalion of the enemy is better than breaking them. By applying this principle, we can understand that winning a hundred times in a hundred battles is not the ultimate achievement. The ultimate achievement is subduing the enemy without fighting.

Therefore, the highest form of war is having broader strategy[5] than the enemy, followed by breaking allies[6] of the enemy, then defeating the enemy in battle[7]. The lowest is to besiege the enemy's city[8]. Siege wars should only be waged if unavoidable. Siege time is very expensive. It takes up to three months to craft and prepare weapons to attack city walls.[9] It takes another three months to build the mounds[10] of construction around the enemy walls. If the general is impatient, he will launch his men to the assault like swarming ants around the citadel so that our troops could lose one third of the casualties while the town still remains untaken. These are dangerous effects of a siege.

Therefore, a skillful leader does not need to use the battlefield to subdue the enemy. He captures the enemy's city without having to attack. He destroys enemy countries without putting his troops in great risk. All is to preserve the force by making use of strategy. Therefore, there is no wear and tear and still there is great benefit. This is the strategy of offensive art.

When deploying the army and we discover that our soldiers are ten times larger than the enemy, then we encircle them. But if we are five times larger, we attack straight up.[11] We divide our troops if we are twice as large.[12] However, if the forces are equal, we make plans to defeat the enemy forces.[13] In situations where the enemy soldiers are more than us, the best thing to do is to avoid direct attacks. If the enemy is too crowded, we retreat completely. So it is better for a small army to persevere rather than be defeated.

The general is the pillar of the nation. If the pillar is solid, the nation is strong. If the pillar is loose, the nation is weak.

We were faced with three challenges. First is that it was unclear if our troops could not advance but we kept them advancing; we were not sure if the troops could back up but we just told them to back up. That's called tying troops. The second challenge is that the position of the internal affairs of the troops was also unclear, but by interfering with the military management, the officers and soldiers would be confused. Thirdly, it was unclear military principle of adaption to circumstances but interfere with the responsibility of commanders, and the generals would be in doubt. If the troops were suspicious and bewildered, the vassal countries would have the opportunity to harass. This is called self-disordered troops and it is to lead others to victory.

In the aspiration of victory, there are five important key elements to observe:

1. Know when to fight and when not if it's going to lead to victory whichever way.

2. Know how to use more troops.

3. Having the same goal and spirit in all ranks will lead to victory.

4. A prepared army will always achieve victory over an unprepared enemy.

5. A talented general who is not restrained by the king will be victorious in battle.

All these five key points, if considered together, are the true path to success.

So we can say that if we know the enemy and know ourselves then we will not be endangered in a hundred battle engagements. If we know ourselves but not the enemy then for every victory gained we will also suffer a defeat. If we know neither the enemy nor ourselves then we will never win.

Chapter 4 – Military Disposition 軍 形

Good generals in the old days first guaranteed their troops could not be defeated and then waited for the enemy to be self-miserable to win the enemy. We are not defeated because of complete preparation. We can win against the enemy because they are vulnerable. So a good fighter creates conditions that makes him formidable. But there is no sure way to make the enemy vulnerable[1] to defeat them.

While we cannot guarantee victory, then we entrench. When we guarantee victory, then we attack. We will entrench because we know we are in a position where victory is uncertain; and we attack because we have more than enough resources to win. Those who are good at entrencing can hide themselves under nine levels of the earth.[2] Those who are good at attacking can attack enemy from nine levels of heaven.[3] In this way, one can fully protect one's own forces and ensure complete victory.

Just seeing the victory that everyone knows is not really good. A victory welcomed by all people is by no means the greatest of victories. We do not need the strength of a giant to lift a feather. We do not need great eyesight to see the sun. Neither do we need great ears to hear thunder. The great fighters of the past not only won the battles but also won very easily.[4] So the victory of the great fighters is not famed for wisdom, nor is it known for bravery. Being prepared for every winning situation is what guarantees a certain victory. This means we are fighting the defeated enemy.

So a great warrior first places himself in the invisible position and then makes sure he does not miss an important opportunity to defeat the enemy. A successful army first ensures invincibility before not missing the enemy's defeat. A winning army first ensures victorious planning before engaging in battle. A defeated army is first fought before victory is achieved. Those who are good at military use must rectify the righteousness and perfect the rules because this is a clue to make certain the decision to either win or lose.

In the art of war, the following should also be considered:

1. Range

2. Measurement

3. Calculation

4. Weigh

5. Victory

The range is a way of determining the terrains of both sides – wide, narrow, long, short.   Then after determining the range, we must measure both sides to know if to use more or less of material resources.   The next course of action is the calculation.   We have to calculate the number of troops on both sides. Then we must weigh our options by determining military strategy, strength and weakness of both sides. After all these have been put into consideration, then it will be easy to know who will achieve the victory and who would be defeated.

Different terrain is so different resources.   Different resources should have different military numbers.   Different military forces bring about different results. A victorious army weighs the "dật[5]" with the "thù[6]", while a defeated army will weigh the "thù" against the "dật".   A victorious army is akin to releasing a flood of water on a high of ten thousand "knotstick[7]" rushed down.   This is referred to as military disposition.

Chapter 5 – Military Force 兵 勢

The principles for controlling a large force are the same as for a small force. The essential element is organization. Commanding a large army to the battlefield is like controlling a small army. It is a matter of formation and information. To keep the whole army from being broken before the attack of the enemy is by using indirect[1] and direct[2] maneuver. In order to make our attacking power like a stone to smash an egg, we must master the magic of real and unreal.[3]

In combat, directly attack the enemy is very obvious; but what brings about victory is the indirect attack on the side.

A general who understands the use of indirect army has an infinite source of tactics like heaven and earth, like rivers and oceans, which will never run out. He's like the sun which shines in the day, and the moon that illuminates at night, diminishing and replenishing, constantly refreshing the cycle of the four seasons. In music, there are only five basic notes, but their variations are infinite. There are only five primary colors[4] but when mixed, their shades and colors are infinite. There are only five basic flavors[5], but their combination creates many unspeakable flavors. In military strategy, however, there are only direct and indirect, but in which they provide an endless range of tactics. Direct and indirect naturally stick together like a spinning wheel.

The rise of floodwaters slowly sweeping away the rock due to erosion – this is an example of military force. The eagle rushes down and snatches its prey in a flash – this is called the moment. In this case, the military force of the skilled fighter is irresistible and the moment is very accurate. Military force is the tension of the bowstring at full stretch; and the moment is when the arrow is released.

In the chaotic situation of the battle, our army seems to be in chaos, but in reality it cannot be chaotic. In the chaotic and tangled situation, the distribution of our troops seems to be disordered, but in reality is invisible. In this way, chaos clearly masks for real organization, cowardice masks for courage, weak force masks for strong force.

The enemy is chaotic because we are organized. The enemy is cowardly because we are courageous. The enemy is weakened because we are strong. Order or disorder is caused by the level of organization. Cowardice or courage is caused by position. Strength or weakness is caused by formation. The skill fighters keep the initiative, use their troops to entice the enemy to chase. We drop small bait to lure the enemy to take and snare to catch them.

Therefore, a skilled general in combat can create a favorable disposition without blaming his subordinates; he knows how to choose talented subordinates that create advantage position. A skilled general will create a force like a rolling stone wood. The nature of the stone wood is quiet on the plane, moving on slope, stopping on square and rolling on circle. So a skilled combating general like rolling round stone wood from ten thousand knobsticks high mountains down to the foot of the mountain. That is exactly military force.

The military force of the skilled warriors is like a round stone wood rolling down from a thousand meter high mountain.

Chapter 6 – Real and Unreal 虛實

As a general principle, the troops that arrive first at the location of the battle and wait for the enemy will have initiative and will be at ease. The troops that arrive later to the battle position will be passive and exhausted. So the great fighters make the enemy come, he is not lured by the enemy.

Making enemies come themselves by luring them to their advantages. Making enemy not to comes by threating harms to them. Using the same principle, if the enemy is leisurely, we disturb them. If the enemy is well-fed, we make them hungry. If the enemy is stationed, we make them move. Attack at points that the enemies have to scramble to protect themselves, and launch lightning attacks on places they did not expect. Our army can travel thousands of miles without getting tired because of getting in an unobstructed place. If we want a certain win, we only attack where enemy cannot defend. In order to be sure of defending, we have to abide in places where the enemy cannot fight.

Therefore, for those who are good at fighting, the enemy will not know where to defend. Those who are good at defending, the enemy won't know where to fight. Delicate instead! So subtle we can make ourselves invisible. Secret instead! So secretive that we can move without making a sound. That's why we keep the fate of the enemy in our palm. We attack but the enemy could not stop because we fight without people. We retreat and the enemy couldn't follow because we escape quickly. But if we want to fight, even though they have deep moats, high fortresses are inescapable because we fight where they have to rescue. If we do not want to fight, we will strike the ground to defend and prevent the enemy from finding us and fighting because we have been suspected of distracting them.

We make the enemy visible and we hide it so we can keep our forces united while the enemy is forced to scatter defenses everywhere. We gathered our troops into one and the enemy had to disperse into ten so the odds were ten against one. Thus our troop is large, the enemy is small. Using a lot of troops to fight a few troops, the clear victory always leans on us at any time.

Because it was impossible to know where we wanted to attack, the enemy had to send defensive troops everywhere. With thinly scattered enemy forces, wherever we want to attack, the enemy troops there will be few. If the enemy defends on the left, the right wing will have few troops. If the enemy tries to defend everywhere, every position will be weakened.

The weak military force is due to defending everywhere. The strong force is because we have the enemy to defend all over the place. We lack troops because we are distributing troops to guard against the enemy. We have more than enough troops because we make the enemy guard us.

If we know the time and place of the battle in advance, we can easily go thousands of miles to arrive to join force at the battlefield to fight. If we do not know the time and location of the battle, we do not know if we should join forces on the front to save troops on the back, the back cannot save the front, the left cannot save the right, the right cannot not save the left. How much more so if our troops are thousands miles apart? Even if they are several miles away, how can we save each other?

According to my expectation in this condition, surpassing in mililitary number is not necessarily the deciding factor of victory or defeat. So the victory is created by us. Even if the enemy is more numerous, we can prevent them from joining the battle to fight us.

Planning is to discover the enemy's intention and also to calculate the matter of victory or loss. We tease the enemy to know and understand the rules of their operation. We lure them to deploy troops where they we can see their combat skill, including their strength and weakness points.   Consider the situation to know if the enemy layout is insufficient or excess troops.

We disguised as cleverly and as invisible for the enemy to not recognize our whereabouts.   Being invisible, the enemy spy has deep underground nor detectable.   Because they could not investigate our whereabouts, the enemy's general does not know how to deal with us.

Everyone realized that we are in a superior position, but no one realized that we depend on the enemy's situation to transform into victory.   People only know how we defeat the enemy, but they don't know how we use that method.   That is why we don't use the same strategy twice, we have to adapt flexibly according to the new situation of the enemy.

Military strategy is like flowing water.   The characteristic of water is to avoid high places but drain into low places.   So victory in the war is due to avoiding strong enemy positions, attacking weak enemy positions. Water depends on the terrain to adapt.   Combat depends on the enemy's situation to arrange.   So there is nothing certain in war as the water never holds a certain form. Therefore, a general who achieves victory by strategizing his tactics based on the changing situation of the enemy is called miraculous.

Of the five elements[1], no element prospers forever.   No season of the four seasons[2] lasts indefinitely.   The sun rises and sets.   Moon rounds and wanes.

Chapter 7 – Maneuvering 軍爭

According to the permission to use soldiers, the general receives orders from the king. It is the job of the general to arrange the available military forces, put soldiers in effective order, build camps and set up battles against enemy. After that, the most difficult task is maneuvering against the enemy. The inherent difficulties in this job are the need to turn curve into straight and turn disadvantages into advantages. So the general can lead the army around using small profits to lure the enemy. Therefore, we arrive at true goal destination before enemy even though we start later. That is the mastery of turning curves into straight.

Bringing troops to maneuvering against the enemy is sometimes beneficial but other times very dangerous. If we wait to gather forces with adequate equipment before attempting to take advantage, we risk coming too late. If we hurry to abandon equipment to take advantage, we risk losing the abandoned equipment. If ordered to force soldiers to march with armor wrapped in military bags, move night and day without rest to double the distance, cross a hundred miles to get to the advantage, the three generals[1] can be arrested. The strong soldiers will come first, the weak ones will come later and only one-tenth of the soldiers will actually arrive to the destination on time. If marched fifty miles, the generals and vanguard forces would be stopped and half the force would come. If marching thirty miles, only two-thirds would come. Therefore, the army that has no equipments must lose, the one with no food must starve, and with no personal supplies must be difficult to live.

Without understanding the vassals' machinations, it was impossible to anticipate the association. The terrain of mountains and forests is not known, so we cannot lead troops there. General must make use of the knowledge of the locals to make the best of the nature's features. So to use the battle army one must rely on improvisation that pretends to act, must rely on the interests that act and depending on the circumstances that improvised. Therefore, the speedy army is as fast as a whirlwind, slowly as dense as the jungle, encroachment is like a burning fire, defense is like a mountain, mystery is like darkness and the attack is like thunder.

Capture the village then distribute that among troops to keep. Expand the territory then divide that benefit to use. Weigh and measure carefully then depending on the situations to take action. Victory belongs to the person who masters the combination of curvature and straightness. That is the way to maneuvering against enemy.

The military book says: in battle, human voices are not strong enough to be heard, which is why we use gongs and trumpets. Our vision is not accurate enough, which is why we use banners and flags. Set up the gongs and trumplets, banners and flags to let the whole army listen with the ears and see with the same eyes and act unanimously. Unified in understanding, the brave cannot move forward alone and the coward does not withdraw himself. This is the art of military management. So in night fighting, the gongs, trumplets and fire are used as signals and in the day, relying on gongs, trumplets, flags and banners to adapt to the ears and eyes of our army.

For the enemy's three troops[2], we should snatch away their morale. As for the enemy's general, we should cast doubt about their determination.

Military morale, when it first arrives, is sharp and strong, after a while it is languid and lazy, and finally wants to return home. Therefore, those who are good at using troops should avoid the morale of the enemy when they first arrive and fight at a time when they want to return home. This is the way that shatters the morale of enemy troops. Take our organized troops, deal with chaotic enemy troops. Take our calmly troops, deal with bewildered enemy troops. This is the way that dissipates the enemy's general determination. Get our near troops to wait for the enemy troops from far away. Get our eased troops to wait for the tired enemy troops. Get our well-fed troops to wait for the hungry enemy troops. This is the way to control military strength. Do not fight with the well organized enemy. Do not fight with the mighty enemy. This is the way to control changes.

Basic principles when using army: do not approach to fight with the enemy troops on a high hill. Do not fight with the enemy troops leaning on a mountain mound. Do not chase with the feint retreated enemy troops. Do not fight with the pungent enemy troops. Do not fight with the lured enemy troops. Do not interfere with the returned home enemy troops. Do not besiege without leaving the exit for enemy troops. Do not press too hard with a desperated enemy troops. This is the art of maneuvering in warfare.

Chapter 8 – Nine Changes 九變

During the war, the general received orders from the king and then arranges the available military forces. The general must know that if the terrain is not favorable, the force must not be stationed. If the roads and communications are good, associate with allies. Do not linger on barren land[1]. If besieged[2], you have to think straight; and situations of life and death[3], risk must be taken. There are roads where we should not step on them.[4] We sometimes do not fight the enemy.[5] We sometimes do not besiege the fortresses.[6] There are places we shouldn't fight.[7] There are even orders from the king that we shouldn't obey.[8]

A general who masters the above nine changes will know how to use his army. A general who does not comprehend these things, even though he knows the terrain, cannot turn them into an advantage terrain for himself. A commander who does not know how to use these nine changes, even if there are five benefits[9], cannot promote the use of military.

The talented one always considers both benefits and harms equally. Considering the disadvantages of a favorable situation, we can certainly achieve our goals. Considering the potential advantages of a dangerous situation, we can find a way to solve our difficulties.

If we want to subdue vassals, then take arms to threaten them. If we want to get vassals to do so, force them into things they cannot help but do. If we want to attract vassals, we must use small profits to buy off.

The principle of using troops is not to rely on the enemy not to fight us but to rely on the available coping tactics. Not relying on the enemy who does not attack us but certainly on the ability to defend our positions.

There are five dangerous drawbacks that often occur to the general: reckless disregard for death will actually lead to death. A living greedy general will be captured. The angry general is easily provoked into enemy superficial action. Self-conceited generals are easy to shame. General who loves the people easily gets troubled. These five are common generals' mistakes and catastrophes to the successful conduct of the war. When the defeated troops and the generals are killed, the reason is not beyond the above five defects. We need to consider them carefully.

Chapter 9 – Marching 行軍

In the matter of marching, camping and observing the movements of enemies in different terrains when going through the mountains and valleys, we choose a high position, rely on the stream[1] and face east to camp. Do not climb up[2] to join the battle on the high ground, we should fight down[3], avoid fighting up. That's what we need to know about mountainous terrain and valleys.

Once we cross the river, we move away from it. If the enemy crosses the river to fight us, we do not fight in the middle of the stream. We can gain the advantage by having half of the enemy force overcome and then attack.[4] Do not attack from the other side of the river bank when the enemy approaches the river. Choose an elevated position to the east to wait and do not confront the enemy upstream.[5] This is how to fight on water.

Get past the salt marsh swamp as quickly as possible and don't linger.[6] If you must fight in such marshes, be stationed in a swamp and rely on the trees behind you. This is how to fight in a salt marsh swamp.

On a flat ground, where it is easy to set up a camp, choose a flat place that is easy to move around, has a high ground to the right and behind, leaving danger ahead for the enemy and safety behind. This is how to base your troops on flat ground.

The above four rules are useful for marching and camping operations. Those were the principles that king Huỳnh Đế[7] had used to conveniently defeat four nearby emperors.

When stopping the army camp, avoid the humid place but high places; also, avoid dark places but bright places. If we raise our troops well and have solid refuge, as well as if we take care of the health of the soldiers and camp on the dry ground, the soldiers will avoid all common diseases. This is a guaranteed formula for victory.

When you come to the hillock or dike, take your place in the sun with the high ground to the right and behind you. This will deploy troops to take full advantage of the terrain.

If the river is high and the water is foaming because of the rain on the source and we want to cross, we wait for the water to decrease.[8]

If you encounter a mountain waterfall, dead end, deep bushes, swamps or narrow streams, you must pay attention and stay away. At the same time, try to force the enemy towards such places, then when we go ahead to fight. The enemy will rely on those places and should be in danger.

Close to where our troops are stationed on hilly lands, where there are reeds or dusty ponds, we search carefully because it is the ideal place for the enemy to ambush. If the enemies nearby are quiet and do not attack, they are confident in the strength that would have taken advantage of the terrain. If the enemy is far away but has come to challenge us to fight, then they are luring us to attack. If the enemy camp seems to be open for attack, that's a trap. If trees and bushes seem to be moving, enemies are coming. If the irregular blocks are gathered to prevent our advance between the reeds and the grass, the enemy is setting a trap. If the birds suddenly fly off from trees, there is an ambush below and the terrified animal running away shows that the enemy wants to fight a surprise face down. If the dust is high and pointed, it is the enemy who comes by horseback. If the dust is low and wide, it means the soldiers are approaching by walking. When the dust spreads in different directions, the enemy is collecting firewood. Small dust clouds moving in and out meant that the enemy is setting up camp.

If the enemy envoys speak humble words while increasing their military preparations, it is a sign that the enemy wants to attack. If the envoys speak in violent languages while their force is driving forward as if to the attack, it is a sign that they are preparing to retreat. If light carriages run out and spread out to the two flanks, it is a sign that the enemy was forming a formation to fight.

If the enemy's troops flock and form, a decisive attack is coming. If the enemy troops seem to be half advancing and half retreating, it is a trap. If enemy soldiers are leaning on their spears then they are hungry. If enemy soldiers go to get some water but drink before bringing it back, they are thirsty.[9] If the enemy could not make use of the obvious opportunities, they would be exhausted. The place where birds gather without disturbance is where there is no enemy barracks. A disturbance in the enemy camp at night means they are scared. The widespread unrest in the enemy troops is caused by a weakness in command. If the flags and banners of the enemy are leaning over, there is disorder among the troops. If the enemy officers are angry and irritable, they are depressed. When enemy troops feed rice to the horses and slaughter animals to eat their meat, and they are not hanging the pots and returning to their tent, they are ready for the final attack. If soldiers are huddled together and whisper among themselves, it is a sign of discontent among the ranks of the soldiers and the commander.

If enemy rewards frequently then they are at the end position of resources. If the enemy punishes frequently, they are in critical condition. If the enemy general is initially fierce towards the soldiers because of fear, it means that the general is ignorant. If the enemy is angry and pulls troops to the battlefield without retreating, we should watch carefully. If we have no advantage in military numbers or a military standoff, then all we need to do is gather our forces in one place, continue to monitor the enemy and increase the troops. A general who is careless by underestimating his enemies will surely be captured.

When the general is trusted by the soldiers even if he punishes them, they will not submit. If, however, the general is admired by his soldiers but he doesn't punish them when appropriate, they will be useless. Therefore, generals must combine soldiers with righteousness and bind them with discipline. This is the path to invincibility.

If the general performs consistency in orders and instructions, the soldiers will be loyal to the general. Without consistency, soldiers won't know where to listen. These are common benefits for both generals and soldiers to maintain consistency.

Chapter 10 – Terrain 地形

Terrain can be classified in this manner: accessible ground, entangled ground, dilapidated ground, narrow ground, dangerous ground and far ground.

Accessible ground is the terrain that any party can come and cross. To keep our upper hand in this terrain, be sure to occupy the high, sunny areas[1] and look into our supply roads. Taking over this terrain first and waiting for the enemy to fight will guarantee victory.

The entangled ground is easy to access but difficult to exit.[2] On such terrain, if the enemy is poorly prepared, it will be easy for us to take risks and defeat them. However, if the enemy is well prepared and our attack fails, it will be difficult for us to return because we are in a serious disadvantage.

If both parties could not gain the upper hand by taking initiative, the terrain is called dilapidated ground.[3] When entering this terrain, although the enemy gives an attractive advantage, we control ourselves by leading our troops away to drag the enemy out. After that, when the enemy troops come out halfway, we will return to attack. This way, it will be more beneficial.

For narrow ground[4], we must make sure to occupy and consolidate the position first, then wait for the enemy to enter. If the enemy has been there first and has had the opportunity to strengthen their position, then we should not fight them. However, if the enemy has not strengthened their position, we should come to consolidate and attack.

When we get to dangerous grounds[5] first, we will be able to occupy high, sunny places where it will be easy for us to observe and wait for the enemy. If the enemy goes there first, we should not fight and we should retreat.

Far ground[6] is a far and wide place. If we enter this terrain and the two parties have equal forces, it is difficult to fight and even if possible, we have no advantage.

Above are the six principles of terrain advantage and it is the primary responsibility of any military commander to consider them carefully.

Military matter has six things that fail. None of that comes from the disaster of heaven and earth[7], but all are the faults of the general. These are fleeing troops[8], insubordination troops, ruined troops, collapsed troops, chaotic troops and routed troops[9].

Soldiers flee because the forces are equal but took one-on-ten so they have to run. Insubordination troops are due to the strong of senior officers and the generals' feeble mindedness. Generals are strong but feeble senior officers are called ruined troops. The collapsed troops are caused by the high-ranking officers getting angry and going on their own without waiting for the above order before the prime minister could assess the chance of success. And the general does not not know the competence of high-ranking officers so the troops would collapse. The chaotic troops are caused by a feeble-minded general that lacks dignity, consistency in command, and the soldiers' disgruntled heart. All this leads to chaotic troops. The general does not accurately assess the enemy's strength, take less against much, take weak against strong, combating lack of military elitepioneers. It is the result of a rout troop.

The six paths mentioned above bring failure. Generals who carry the responsibility of their troop must consider these factors and find a way to work around them.

Terrain is a supportive element for maneuver. The ability to accurately assess the enemy's situation in which the army is set to prevail, calculate obstacles, dangerous positions, and distances near or far, this is the path of generals. If we understand all these and apply them in reality, the general will definitely win. If neither understands nor practices, the general will be defeated.

Therefore, after analyzing the rules of the war and seeing all things that only lead to victory, the generals must fight, even if the king does not order. Similarly, generals must know when to refuse a king's order to fight if the signs aren't just for victory. A general who advances without coveting fame and retreats without fear of committing crimes[10] but only thinking of protecting the people and benefiting the king, such generals are truly an invaluable treasure of the nation.

If we treat soldiers like children we can lead them into abyss. By treating soldiers like beloved children, they will stand by us to death. However, if we indulge them but cannot use them, love them but cannot command them, and we refuse to punish them for their crimes, then these soldiers will become useless like spoiled children. The general cannot lead this army to battle.

Knowing that our troops can fight without knowing the conditions that can beat the enemy or not, the victory is only half. Knowing the situation that the enemy can fight without knowing whether our military situation can fight the enemy or not, the victory is only half. Knowing the readiness of both enemies and our troops, but not knowing the nature of the terrain, the victory is still only half. Therefore, those who know how to hold the army do not mislead, the soldiers who fight will not be in danger. Those are the reasons why we say: by knowing the enemy and knowing ourselves, then we will surely win. If we know the atmosphere and the terrain then we will win completely.

Chapter 11 – Nine Ground Positions 九地

In military use, there are nine ground positions: dispersed ground position, shoal groundposition, contested ground position, allocated ground position, linked ground position, important ground position, difficult ground position, besieged ground position, and death ground position.

Fighting on our own land is called dispersed ground position.[1] Taking a short distance into enemy land and fighting is called shoal ground position.[2] The land that is beneficial to any party occupying is the contested ground position.[3] The land that is easily accessible for both parties is called allocated groundposition. The land that connects the border with the three countries, whoever takes it first, is joined by those three countries to be called linked ground position. Deep into the enemy land with many cities occupied behind us is important ground position. Mountains, rugged cliffs, swamps, and wetlands, all hard to cross areas are difficult ground position. The entrance is narrow, there is no way to retreat, so a small force could easily defeat a large force is besieged ground position. If we have to fight to hope for survival and the delay of a certain moment will cause disaster is death ground position.

Therefore, it is not recommended to fight on dispersed ground position[4], do not linger on shoal ground position[5], do not attack on contested ground position[6], arrange the battlefield and maintain contact on allocated ground position, partnership with all vassals on linked ground position, take the opportunity to occupy food on important ground position[7], quickly overcome difficult ground position[8], use cunning tactics when on besieged ground position[9], and on death ground position, fight hard.[10]

So, in the old days, skilled fighters could make the enemy front and rear forces losing contact.   Small troops and large troops cannot rely on each other. The general and the troops lose touch. Officers and soldiers cannot help each other. Soldiers are separated, unable to gather. The formation is in disorder. Therefore, if someone who is good at using soldiers sees an opportubity, he will fight; if not, he will halt.

Dare to ask: What if the enemy pulls troops to attack us with a large and well trained army? Answer: Win first the most favorable condition of the enemy, then they will listen to us.[11]

The precious element of military operations is speed. Take advantage when the enemy is not ready, march on unexpected routes and fight the places where they are not taking precautions.

Military plays a guest in the enemy country. If we go deep into enemy territory, the more united our troops will be, making it harder for the host to overcome us. If we find fertile fields, then take them and use them to feed your troops. You have to bolster the morale of your soldiers so as to keep their spirits and preserve their vitality. Do not make them do anything in vain.

When in motion, use strange tricks to keep the enemy from guessing your tactics. Let the troops go into dangerous places, they would risk their life to fight hard because they could not retreat. If the soldiers would risk their lives to fight then nothing will bother them. All ranking soldiers will make every effort and no longer fear in that situation. So your army will show the will to fight a united front when in no other way and fight to the last.

Such an army would not need to emend its team to remain alert, no need to ask if they still fulfill their mission. Even without encouraging them, they will still stick together and support each other, without order they will still obey because they are disciplined. Prohibiting all practices of divination and superstition as well as eliminating suspicions in the army, then such soldiers will die without changing their hearts.

Our soldiers are not abundant, not because of contempt of wealth, nor regret for the life because they hate life. On the day of departure, those who sit are crying with tears soaked in their shirts, those who lie are crying tears on their cheeks. But once at a time of no return, they will show the courage of the Chuyên Chư[12] and the bravery of Tào Quế[13].

The person who knows how to use his troops is like the Suất Thiên[14], the famous snake in Hoành Sơn mountain. If we attack on the head, it attacks back with its tail. If we attack the tail, it attacks back with its head. If we attack the middle part, it attacks back with both its head and tail.

Someone asked: Can soldiers imitate Suất Thiên with their army? Answer: Yes! The people of Wu and Yuet did not like each other, but when they sat in a boat across the river, encountering strong winds and waves, they save each other as their right hand helped the left.

So tying the horse legs, burying the chariot wheels for soldiers determined to fight is not enough to believe. We must urge all the soldiers to apply their military training bravely. Force soft or hard, weak or strong are promoting the forte for taking advantage of terrain. So, skilled generals lead the troops in their hands as if leading a single person that soldiers cannot help but follow.

The strategy of the general must be deep and discreet, he must use tricks and gossip to keep soldiers in the dark to mask his true intentions. A general should change his layout and plans so that soldiers don't know what he's doing. The general should change his location and lead his army around so that soldiers cannot predict his plans.

When the general orders the soldiers into battle, he shouldn't block their way, he should not be the stumbling block on their path to victory, like a person who climbs very high and then kickes the ladder away. The general leads his troops deep into enemy territory, burning boats and smashing pots to promote morale of soldiers like a herder of goats, herding forth then going ahead and herding side then going horizontal. Soldiers don't need to know where to go.

Navigating and leading soldiers into danger is the job of the general. Adaptive improvisation to nine types of ground, assess the dangers of attacking or retreating and understand the mood of soldiers. This is what the general should carefully consider.

The principle of combat in the role of guest in the enemy country is the deeper into the enemy land, the more solid the troops will be. If we are too close to our borders, the soldiers will disperse. When we lead our army across our borders, we enter the secluded land. If the territory is accessible from all four directions, it is allocated ground. If we penetrate deeply into enemy territory, it is important ground. If we only go a short distance into enemy territory, it is called shoal ground. If the enemy is entrenched behind and there are narrow paths ahead of us, that is the besieged ground. When we don't have a way out, it's death ground.

Therefore, in the dispersed ground, we unify the will of the soldiers. At the shoal ground, we communicate closely with the soldiers. At the contested ground, we follow the enemy closely. At allocated ground, we defend. At the linked ground, we strengthen the alliance. In important ground, we protect the food of soldiers. In difficult ground, we try to overcome. At the besieged ground, we block all entrances and exits. In the death ground, we let the soldiers choose the only remaining path between life and death. So we understand the nature of soldiers is to resist being surrounded, forced too much will risk death, and on command when in danger.

Without understanding the strategy of the vassals we cannot take into account the association. The terrain of forests, point of stations, caves, swamps, and canals is not known then do not leading troops there. Without scouting, you cannot gain ground advantage. If the general does not understand even one of the basic above principles of war, he is not a general worthy of his authority.

A worthy general, when attacking a strong country, makes the enemy army unable to mobilize to concentrate forces. We threatened to overwhelm the enemy that other countries could not rescue. Therefore, it is not necessary to fight diplomatic relations with vassals, as well as from the need to strengthen one's power in vassal countries. We only keep our own strength to threaten the enemy. Therefore, we can raze the village and destroy the capital of the enemy.

We give reward without according to the rules, give orders without according to the rules, commanding the entire army as dictating a person. Assigning work to soldiers, not stating the tactics and sending soldiers into dangerous places without showing harm. Launch troops into danger places to turn danger into peace. Launch troops into a dangerous sieged places to turn death into life and win.

So, in carrying out military operations, we pretend to follow the will of the enemy while actually pushing our troops fighting in one direction. This way even thousands of miles will not save their generals from our swords. This is how we use our talents and cunning to achieve our goals.

On the day the war is declared, blockade of the border, cancellation of the covenant, banning of all information and travel of enemy ambassadors. Reviewing the plan discreetly in the temple and carefully arranging the work. If the enemy has a loophole, then we intervene. Take what they value most and limit them with time. Revise the plan according to the enemy's situation until we can bring the enemy to our decisive battle.

So, before the battle, our troops are calm and discreet, shy like a virgin until the enemy showed an opening. At that time, we attack with a speed like an opening cage rabbit so that the enemy has no opportunity to fight back.

Chapter 12 – Fire Attack 火攻

There are five ways to attack enemies with fire. First is to burn enemy troops. Second is to burn enemy food storage. Third is to burn enemy vehicles. Fourth is to burn enemy weapons. Fifth is to burn enemy team.

Fire attacking needs conditions and preparation in advance. To use fire, one must consider the weather of the season and choose the right day. A favoured season is when the weather is dry and the appropriate days are when the moon is in the constellations of the Cơ, Bích, Dực or Chẩn.[1] These are four days with strong winds blowing at night.

When using firepower, we must know flexible improvisation for five cases. If the fire is burning in the enemy camp then we must hurry and respond from the outside.[2] When the fire is burning and the enemy is not chaotic, then do not rush to attack immediately.[3] Wait until the fire has wide spread and see if it can actually strike and act accordingly. Firing from the outside into the enemy barracks does not need to wait for internal effects; we have to rely on the upwind to attack, not attacking at the downwind.[4] The wind blows all day then easily stops at night. The military man should be familiar with the five instances of fire and be prepared accordingly.

By using fire to attack, the effect is clearly visible. Using water to attack makes the army position stronger. Water can be used to block rather than destroy enemy equipments and supplies.

After winning the battle and capturing the enemy stronghold without rewarding the soldiers, it is a disaster. This is called ballast loss. Therefore, the wise lord and the loyal general should know how to take care and arrange these things.

Don't move unless you see a clear advantage. Do not use soldiers unless there is something to gain. Do not fight if we are not in danger. The king cannot mobilize army because of personal anger. The general cannot engage in battle because of personal outrage. Only mobilize army if it is beneficial for the country, otherwise do not move. Anger can turn into satisfaction and outrage can turn into joy, but a country that has been destroyed is hard to recover and cannot give life to those who have died. Therefore a head of state needs to be vigilant and a loyal general should be on guard. This is the way to keep a peaceful country and an intact army.

Chapter 13 – Using Spy 用間

Raising hundred thousand soldiers[1] and marching them thousands of miles away. All costs of hundreds of families and public funds[2] to suffer each day up to thousand taels of gold. There will be widespread disruption at home and abroad, people will be strenuously exhausted on the roadside, neglecting daily work of up to seventy thousand houses.[3]

Spending years to win in a day without daring to spend hundred taels of silver on spies to discover an enemy's situation. This is terribly inhumane. This is not the behavior of a leader for the people, nor is it worthy of being an assisstant for ruler or a master of victory.

For what allows a leader and a general to attack decisively and successfully, where ordinary people fail, is foreknowledge. Foreknowledge cannot be found by consulting with the divine being[4] or by comparing similar situations. Nor could it be found by measuring the movements of heaven and earth but were obtained from people who had accurate knowledge of the enemy's situation.

In this respect, there are five types of spies that we can use: local spy, internal spy, counterspy, suicide spy and reported spy. If we use all five types, no one can understand our scheme. It is a type of sacred organization and the greatest treasure of a wise ruler.

Local spies are recruited from enemy peasants.[5] Internal spies are from enemy court officials.[6] Counter spying means using the enemy's own spies against them.[7] Suicide spies[8] are people who are given false information to take for spies by enemies. Reported spies[9] are the ones who focus on bringing enemy information report to us.

So in the whole army, no one is closer to us than spies. No one is more rewarded than spying. No secret is more closely protected than the spy network. Spies must be used wisely and treated with kindness and virtue. We must use the utmost subtlety to ensure accurate reporting from spies. Subtlety is the key. There are no instances where spy cannot be used.

If a spy reveals information before executing the plan, then both spy and people who known must be put to death. Whether we want to destroy an army, attack a city or assassinate someone, the first important thing is to determine the name of the commander-in-chief, trusted people, assistants, gatekeepers and his bodyguards. We have to order the spy to find out for this information.

When we discover the spy of the enemy who is watching us, we bribe them, take care of them wholeheartedly and release them freely. That way, we can use them as counter spies. Through these spies, we can recruit local spies and internal spies. Through them our death spies will provide false reports to the enemy. And also through them our reported spies will be able to act as needed.

A wise king must know how to use all five types of spies and this knowledge must necessarily come from a counter spy. So we reward the most to counter agent. In ancient times, when the Ân Dynasty revolted, Y Doãn[10] was on the land of Hạ to investigate and when the Zhou revolt, Khương Tử Nha[11] was on the land of Ân's house to investigate.

A wise king or a sage general should choose only the smartest people to act as his spies, then he will surely achieve great things. This is the necessity of battle action and the army depends on it to act.

Notes

Chapter One: The Drawing Board

1. "Soil Types." *Boughton*, https://www.boughton.co.uk/products/topsoils/soil-types/. Accessed 5 December 2020.

2. "Soil Texture." *Queensland Government*, https://www.qld.gov.au/environment/land/management/soil/soil-properties/texture. Accessed 6 December 2020.

3. "Definition of heavy soil." *Dave's Garden*, https://davesgarden.com/guides/terms/go/443/. Accessed 6 December 2020.

4. *Ut supra*, 1

5. Peter Brodie. "The Four Seasons Of Business: Why Spring Is Around The Corner." Forbes, 18 June 2020.

6. Ibid

7. Ibid

8. Statistics by *Statista* showed that the number of students impacted by school closure rose from about 0.3 billion on 25 February 2020 to 1.38 billion on 23 March 2020. These figures referred to learners in pre-primary, primary, lower-secondary, and upper-secondary, and tertiary levels of education.

    Source: Cathy Li and Farah Lalani. "The COVID-19 pandemic has changed online education forever. This is how." World Economic Forum, 29 April 2020.

9. Ibid

10. Nataly E. Yousef. "Coronavirus Economy: These Five Industries Are Currently Thriving." *NoCamels*, 15 March 2020. https://nocamels.com/2020/03/coronavirus-economy-5-industries-thriving/. Accessed 7 December 2020.

11. "Global Fastest Declining Industries by Revenue Growth (%) in 2020." *IBISWorld*, https://www.ibisworld.com/global/industry-trends/fastest-declining-industries/. Accessed 8 December 2020.

12. The airline cut more than 3,500 jobs to stay afloat amid the pandemic.

     Source: Dominic Rushe. "Virgin Atlantic files for bankruptcy protection as Covid continues to hurt airlines." The Guardian, 4 August 2020.

13. The companies were Mitsubishi, Mitsui, Sumitomo, Itochu, and Marubeni. Buffett also invested in Barrick Gold—a Canada-based mining company that produces gold and copper—and Dominion Energy's natural gas transmission and storage business.

     Source: David Ricketts. "What Warren Buffett's Covid-19 bets tell us about investment in a crisis." Financial News, 4 September 2020.

14. Kimberly Amadeo.   "Strategies and Examples of Trading Sideways." *The Balance*, 11 November 2020.

15. People invested their savings into OneCoin. In Britain, people spent over 30 million euros on OneCoin in the first six months of 2016. Between 2014 and 2017, over 4 billion euros have been invested in many countries like Pakistan, Brazil, Norway, Canada, Yemen, and Palestine.

     Source: "Cryptoqueen: How this woman scammed the world, then vanished." BBC, 24 November 2019.

16. Nick Statt. "Pokemon Go never went away — 2019 was its most lucrative year." *The Verge*, 10 January 2020.

17. Marty Hudson. "Do You Tweet — Or Is Twitter Just A Passing Fad?" *MedicalGPS*, 8 December 2009. https://blog.medicalgps.com/do-you-tweet-or-is-twitter-just-a-passing-fad/. Accessed 8 December 2020.

18. "Is Twitter a Fad?" Canadian Marketing Association, 20 May 2009. https://www.the-cma.org/about/blog/is-twitter-a-fad. Accessed 8 December 2020.

19. Sam Jordan. "Why Twitter is a Fad." *The Better Blog*, 29 January 2013. https://mediashower.com/blog/why-twitter-is-a-fad/. Accessed 8 December 2020.

20. Commenting on the outcome of his prediction, Stoll said: "Of my many mistakes, flubs, and howlers, few have been as public as my 1995 howler. Wrong? Yep... Now, whenever I think I know what's happening, I temper my thoughts: Might be wrong, Cliff..."

    Source: Sam Parr. "Newsweek in 1995: Why the Internet Will Fail?" The Hustle, 21 December 2015.

21. Merriam-Webster (n.d.). Disruption. In *Merriam-Webster Dictionary*. https://www.merriam-webster.com/dictionary/disruption. Accessed 9 December 2020.

22. Caroline Howard. "Disruption Vs. Innovation: What's The Difference?" *Forbes*, 27 March 2013.

23. "Largest stock exchange operators worldwide as of Mar 2020, by market capitalization of listed companies." *Statista*, 23 November 2020.

24. Warren Venketas. "Forex Market Size: A Trader's Advantage." *DailyFX*, 15 January 2019.

25. Raynor de Best. "Market capitalization of cryptocurrencies from 2013 to 2019." *Statista*, 25 November 2020.

26. Avery Hartmans. "Jeff Bezos just turned 57. Here's how he built Amazon into a $1.56 trillion company and became the world's richest person." *Business Insider*, 12 January 2021.

27. "14 Different Types of Terrain." *Nayturr*, https://nayturr.com/types-of-terrain/. Accessed 10 December 2020.

28. Larry Kim. "5 Entrepreneurs Who Ignored Their Advisers and Became Wildly Rich." *Inc.*, 5 May 2015.

29. Ibid

30. Patrick J. Kiger. "9/11: Six Tech Advances to Prevent Future Attacks." *National Geographic News*, 9 September 2011.

31. Neil Patel. "7 Ways to Prove You're Trustworthy as an Entrepreneur." *Entrepreneur*, 1 June 2016.

Chapter Two: The Attack

1. Betsy Mikel. "1 Personality Trait Steve Jobs Always Looked For When Hiring for Apple." *Inc.*, 11 December 2017.

2. Ibid

3. Ibid

4. Tom Huddleston Jr. "These are Bill Gates' 2 superpowers, according to Bill Gates." *CNBC,* 9 October 2019.

5. Sarah Boseley. "How Bill and Melinda Gates helped save 122m lives – and what they want to solve next." *The Guardian*, 14 February 2017.

6. Stephanie Watson. "2020 Lifetime Achievement: Bill and Melinda Gates." *WebMD*, 4 February 2020.

7.   Donna Fenn. "9 Brutal Startup Mistakes That Can Kill Your Business (and How to Avoid Them)." *American Express*, 2 September 2014.

8.   Esha Chhabra. "How This Women-Led Ice Cream Brand Shook Up The Industry." *Forbes*, 30 March 2019.

9.   *Ut supra*, 7

10.   Tim Smith. "Qualitative Analysis." *Investopedia*, 15 May 2020.

11.   "Real Life Examples of Qualitative Forecasting." https:// smallbusiness.chron.com/real-life-examples-qualitative-forecasting-72990.html, 12 October 2020. Accessed 10 January 2021.

12.   Ibid

13.   Ibid

14.   *Ut supra*, 10

15.   Ibid

16.   Norman Marks. "Are Your Business Decisions Failing Because They Are Biased?" *CMSWire*, 13 September 2019. www.cmswire.com/ information-management/are-your-business-decisions-failing-because-they-are-biased/. Accessed 18 January 2021.

17.   "Quantitative Analysis." *Corporate Financial Institute*, https:// corporatefinanceinstitute.com/resources/knowledge/finance/ quantitative-analysis/. Accessed 19 January 2021.

18.   Andrew Zaleski. "7 businesses that cloned others and made millions." *CNBC*, 4 October 2017.

19.   Ibid

20.   Kimberlee Leonard. "Examples of Quantitative Reasoning for a Business." https://smallbusiness.chron.com/examples-quantitative-reasoning-business-30966.html, 5 November 2018. Accessed 19 January 2021.

21.   Shaun Snapp. "The Missed Opportunity of Causal Forecasting?" *Brightwork Research & Analysis*, https://www.brightworkresearch.com/the-missed-opportunity-of-causal-forecasting/, 3 October 2010. Accessed 20 January 2021.

22.   Chris Morris. "10 iconic US companies that have left America." *CNBC*, 21 April 2016.

23.   "The Best and Worst Countries for Business: Ease of doing business ranking." *Wall Street Journal*, 2018. https://graphics.wsj.com/table/DoingBusiness. Accessed 20 January 2021.

24.   World Bank Group. "Doing Business 2020–Sustaining the pace of reforms." *World Bank Group*, 24 October 2019.

25.   Legal Team New Zealand. "Politics and Business: What Does It Mean For New Zealand in 2019?" *Biz Latin Hub*, https://www.bizlatinhub.com/politics-business-new-zealand-2019/, 25 April 2019.

26.   Ibid

27.   Endy M. Bayuni. "When business and government mix too well in Indonesia." *The Jakarta Post*, 28 November 2018.

28.   Ibid

29.   "Economic influence on business activity." *BBC UK*, https://www.bbc.co.uk/bitesize/guides/zjjnnrd/revision/1. Accessed 20 January 2021.

30.   Ibid

31. "The economy and business." *BBC UK*, https://www.bbc.co.uk/bitesize/guides/zrwtmfr/revision/2#:~:text=This%20downturn%20in%20economic%20activity,increase%20when%20unemployment%20is%20higher. Accessed 21 January 2021.

32. "Facebook, Google and Microsoft 'avoiding $3bn in tax in poorer nations'." *BBC*, 26 October 2020.

33. Jemima McEvoy. "Eskimo Pie Becomes Edy's Pie: Here Are All The Brands That Are Changing Racist Names And Packaging." *Forbes*, 26 June 2020.

34. Michael Hogan. "How cancel culture is affecting business." *Smart Company*, 9 July 2019.

35. Jack Kelly. "Wayfair Employees' Protest Of Sales To Detention Centers Could Backfire On Them." *Forbes*, 2 July 2019.

36. Ibid

37. Ibid

38. *Ut supra*, 34

39. *Ut supra*, 35

40. Kweilin Ellingrud. "The Upside Of Automation: New Jobs, Increased Productivity And Changing Roles For Workers." *Forbes*, 23 October 2018.

41. Samuel D. Brickley and Brian M. Gottesman. *Business Law Basics*. http://www.businesslawbasics.com/business-law-basics. Accessed 25 January 2021.

42. "China remains a top investment priority for 60 percent of foreign companies, despite a challenging year for growth and profitability." *Bain and Company*, https://www.bain.com/about/

media-center/press-releases/2016/amcham-china-business-survey-bain-2016/, 20 January 2016. Accessed 25 January 2021.

43. "Insights on handling coronavirus from an earlier report on business and outbreaks." *World Economic Forum*, 11 March 2020.

Chapter Three: The Strategy

1. Pauline Meyer. "Apple Inc's Generic Strategy & Intensive Growth Strategies." *Panmore Institute*, 5 June 2019. http://panmore.com/apple-inc-generic-strategy-intensive-growth-strategies#:~:text=Apple%20Inc.'s%20generic%20strategy%20is%20broad%20differentiation.,stands%20out%20in%20the%20market. Accessed 15 December 2020.

2. In terms of safety, it was reported that Tesla's Model S was the safest car ever tested by the National Highway Traffic Safety Administration. It earned top marks across all categories.

    Source: Michael Kern. "Why Are Tesla Cars So Popular?" *Yahoo! Finance*, 28 March 2020.

3. Tesla owners agree with this. Tesla's technology includes an autopilot feature, over-the-air updates, charger location, almost full driver control of car features, and so on. It has been described as The Car of the Future.

    Source: ibid

4. "Global Smartphone Market Share: By Quarter." *Counterpoint*, 20 November 2020. https://www.counterpointresearch.com/global-smartphone-share/. Accessed 15 December 2020.

5. "Apple's iPhone revenue from 3rd quarter 2007 to 4th quarter 2020." *Statista*, October 2020.

Chapter Four: The Mystery

1. Annie Palmer. "Amazon is on a hiring spree amid widespread coronavirus layoffs and record unemployment." *CNBC*, 9 September 2020.

2. Jay Greene. "Amazon now employs more than 1 million people." *The Washington Post*, 29 October 2020.

Chapter Five: The Winning Team

1. "The Worst War Crimes Ever Imaginable." *All That's Interesting*, 2 June 2016. https://allthatsinteresting.com/worst-war-crimes-in-history/. Accessed 12 October 2020.

2. The United States, in a bid to be ahead of the Soviet Union in global weaponry, chose to give these perpetrators immunity in exchange for the information gathered during the experiments.

   Source: ibid

3. "Trade Secrets: 10 of the Most Famous Examples." *Vethan Law Firm, P. C.*, 11 August 2016. https://info.vethanlaw.com/blog/trade-secrets-10-of-the-most-famous-examples. Accessed 16 December 2020.

4. Chuck Price. "17 Great Search Engines You Can Use Instead of Google." Search Engine Journal, 5 April 2020. https://www.searchenginejournal.com/alternative-search-engines/271409/#close. Accessed 16 December 2020.

5. *Ut supra*, 3

6. ibid

7. ibid

8. ibid

9.   Paul A. Argenti. "When Should Your Company Speak Up About a Social Issue?" *Harvard Business Review*, 16 October 2020.

10.   Ibid

11.   Data sourced from Yahoo Finance.

Chapter Six: The Early Bird

1.   Gary stated that another reason why TikTok became so popular was that it targeted younger audiences.

      Source: Gary Vaynerchuk.   "Why The TikTok (Formerly Musical.ly) App Is So Important." *Gary Vaynerchuk*, 2018. https://www.garyvaynerchuk.com/why-tiktok-formerly-musical-ly-app-is-important/. Accessed 17 December 2020.

2.   Carl Franzen. "The History Of The Walkman: 35 Years Of Iconic Music Players." *The Verge*, 1 July 2014.

3.   Alexandra Appolonia.   "How BlackBerry went from controlling the smartphone market to a phone of the past." *Business Insider*, 21 November 2019.

4.   ibid

5.   Victoria Ahl. "4 Clever Ways These Companies Poached Talent From Their Competitors." *LinkedIn*, 19 July 2017.

6.   Ibid

Chapter Seven: The Unpredictable Maneuver

1.   Andy Gregory. "Coronavirus: Bar condemned for offering deals on Corona beer 'while the pandemic lasts.'" *Independent*, 3 February 2020.

2.   The bar responded to the outrage with a follow-up post which read: "Let's be honest, there are worse things you can catch in

Hamilton." John Lawrenson, the CEO of the company that owns the bar, saw the outrage as a good thing for his company. He was quoted to have said, "The great thing about living in today's society is that there is a small but loud minority of people who get offended by everything and I can always rely on them to get triggered. So I'd just like to say thanks to all the snowflakes for the free advertising and thanks to everyone else with a sense of humour who liked the post."

Source: ibid

3.   ibid

4.   David Z. Morris.   "Coursera offers free online courses to universities worldwide during coronavirus pandemic." *Fortune*, 12 March 2020.

5.   These courses taught on how to stay productive, build relationships when you're not face-to-face, use virtual meeting tools, and balance family and work dynamics in a healthy way.

Source: Blake Morgan.   "50 Ways Companies Are Giving Back During The Coronavirus Pandemic." *Forbes*, 17 March 2020.

6.   ibid

7.   (1) By offering free courses to universities worldwide, Coursera showcased their vision of creating a future where everyone would have access to world-class education. And this wasn't halted by the pandemic. Despite the pandemic, Coursera achieved its aim of empowering people with education that will improve their lives, the lives of their families, and the communities they live in. (2) Likewise, LinkedIn, by giving out its courses for free, maintained its vision of creating economic opportunity for every member of the global workforce. The pandemic period was a time where many lost access to economic opportunities, but through LinkedIn they were taught how to

regain this access, even from the comfort of their homes. (3) Part of the code of ethics of Dolce & Gabbana is Responsibility. And what better way to show responsibility to global health if not by funding research that would look into getting a cure for an incurable disease with a high mortality rate. (4) Giorgio Armani has a corporate social responsibility to support humanitarian projects that are in line with its value.

8.   Michelle Greenwald. "20 Ways Apple Masters Customer Touchpoints And Why It's Great For Business." *Forbes*, 21 May 2014.

9.   Jeff Wiener. "9 Proven Ways to Beat The Competition in Business and Create a Winning Competitive Advantage." *The Kickass Entrepreneur*, 9 December 2020.

      https://www.thekickassentrepreneur.com/beat-the-competition/. Accessed 18 December 2020.

10.   "The 50 greatest business rivalries of all time." *Fortune*, 21 March 2013.

11.   Devika Pawar. "Nike Air Jordan's Journey From Struggling In The NBA To Making Billions Per Year." *Republicworld.com*, 20 May 2020. https://www.republicworld.com/sports-news/basketball-news/nike-air-jordans-journey-to-making-billions-per-year-the-last-dance.html. Accessed 18 December 2020.

12.   Vivian Giang. "3 Keys To Destroying Your Competition." *Forbes*, 24 February 2013.

13.   Ibid

Chapter Eight: The Contingencies

1.   Daphne Blake. "100 Reasons NOT To Start A Business." *Hubworks*, https://hubworks.com/blog/reasons-not-start-business.html, 2 February 2017. Accessed 22 January 2021.

2. "Famous companies that still aren't profitable." https://www.lovemoney.com/gallerylist/91226/famous-companies-that-not-profitable, 10 January 2020. Accessed 23 January 2021.

3. Tanvir Zafar. "10 Successful Entrepreneurs Stories About Getting Through Tough Times." *Life Hack*, https://www.lifehack.org/837974/successful-entrepreneurs-stories. Accessed 23 January 2021.

4. ibid

5. Perrie Kapernaros. "How Competitive Collaboration Can Boost Your Business." *Foundr*, 28 November 2020.

6. ibid

7. Brianne Garrett. "Why Collaborating With Your Competition Can Be A Great Idea." *Forbes*, 19 September 2019.

8. It was commonly believed that human beings have 6 basic emotions—happiness, sadness, fear, anger, surprise, and disgust. But a study led by Alan S. Cowen and Dacher Keltner PhD from the University of California, Berkeley, puts the number at 27. The emotions as outlined by the study are admiration, adoration, aesthetic appreciation, amusement, anxiety, awe, awkwardness, boredom, calmness, confusion, craving, disgust, empathetic pain, entrancement, envy, excitement, fear, horror, interest, joy, nostalgia, romance, sadness, satisfaction, sexual desire, sympathy, and triumph.

   Source: Katie Avis-Riordan. "There are actually 27 human emotions, new study finds." CountryLiving, 11 September 2017. https://www.countryliving.com/uk/wellbeing/news/a2454/27-human-emotions-new-study/#:~:text=In%20previous%20thought%2C%20it%20was,is%20as%20many%20as%2027. Accessed 18 December 2020.

9. Gwen Moran. "Are You a Risk-Taker or Just Reckless?" *Entrepreneur*, 7 October 2013.

10. ibid

11. ibid

12. ibid

13. ibid

14. Anastasia Belyh. "Too Much Funding Can Kill Your Business." *Cleverism*, 19 September 2019. https://www.cleverism.com/too-much-funding-can-kill-business/. Accessed 19 December 2020.

15. ibid

16. ibid

17. Kayla Matthews. "10 Ways Greed Can Ruin Your Business." *Business 2 Community*, 7 May 2014. https://www.business2community.com/leadership/10-ways-greed-can-ruin-business-0875704. Accessed 19 December 2020.

18. "15 Famous Mentoring Relationships." *PUSHfar*, https://www.pushfar.com/article/15-famous-mentoring-relationships/. Accessed 19 December 2020.

19. Neil Patel. "10 Ways You Can Use Your Anger to Build Your Business." *Forbes*, 24 June 2016.

20. Merriam-Webster (n.d.). Self-conceit. In *Merriam-Webster Dictionary*. https://www.merriam-webster.com/dictionary/self-conceit. Accessed 19 December 2020.

21. Merriam-Webster (n.d.). Self-confidence. In *Merriam-Webster Dictionary*. https://www.merriam-webster.com/dictionary/self-confidence. Accessed 19 December 2020.

22. Merriam-Webster (n.d.).   Confidence.   In *Merriam-Webster Dictionary*.   https://www.merriam-webster.com/dictionary/confidence. Accessed 19 December 2020.

23. "End of the line: CEOs who quit their jobs." *The Economic Times*, 28 November 2019.

24. Institutional arrogance. *In Urban Dictionary*, 9 February 2020. https://www.urbandictionary.com/define.php?term=Institutional%20arrogance. Accessed 19 December 2020.

25. The CEOs were reluctant to launch products that could compete favorably with those of Apple and Google. By the time they were ready to take up the challenge, it was already too late. Apple's iPhone and Google's Android had taken a huge chunk of the smartphone market.

     Source: "Personally Disrupted: 14 CEOs Who Got Axed After Failing To Navigate Disruption." *CBInsights*, 17 July 2019. https://www.cbinsights.com/research/ceo-disruption/#blackberry. Accessed 19 December 2020.

Chapter Nine: The Resilience

1. Oliver Rowe. "How leaders can build business resilience." *Financial Management*, 11 March 2020.   https://www.fm-magazine.com/news/2020/mar/how-to-build-business-resilience-coronavirus-response-23121.html.   Accessed 26 January 2021.

2. Martin Reeves and Kevin Whitaker. "A Guide to Building a More Resilient Business." *Harvard Business Review*, 2 July 2020.

Chapter Ten: Using Spies

1. Josh Fruhlinger. "What is corporate espionage? Inside the murky world of private spying." *CSO*, https://www.csoonline.com/

article/3285726/what-is-corporate-espionage-inside-the-murky-world-of-private-spying.html#:~:text=Corporate%20espionage%20%E2%80%94%20sometimes%20also%20called,to%20get%20information%20about%20another, 2 July 2018. Accessed 23 January 2021.

2. ibid

3. Tony Tran. "What is Social Listening, Why it Matters, and 10 Tools to Make it Easier." *Hootsuite*, 3 March 2020.

4. ibid

5. ibid

Compliment Notes

(The Law of War)

Chapter 1 – Planning 始計

1. The two words 始計 (Shǐ jì) in Sino-Vietnamese dictionary mean starting, first or calculating, estimating or planning. I think the word planning is easier to understand and more accurate because people often plan things first and then act (let alone Sun Vu was a person with a deep sharp systematic strategic mind).

2. The ancient versions often translated as heaven or God in the sense of "heavenly time" or God meant the ruler of mankind. But the word 道 (Đạo) means the path or in Lao Tzu's literal sense as the old translations often wrote. However, who understands the Taoist word 道 (Đạo) of Lao Tzu. I think the word righteousness is best used because in ancient Vietnamese, it means "the will of people was the will of God". Besides, we see Sun Vu use this word in that sense throughout the thirteen chapters he wrote. I use the word righteousness in the meaning of Lao Tzu.

3. Flexibly improvably is the use of improvisation to deal with unusual or unexpected events that occur during a war.

4. At the time of Sun Vu in two thousand five hundred years ago, the king and his advisers and generals often divination instead of calculating. They used the method of "yin-yang" or hexagram of bamboo or tortoise shell to ask the god for the plan and if over sixty percent is won and if under sixty percent is lost. But Sun Vu at that time knew how to calculate based on facts to discuss the plan for win or loss. What a transcendent mind!

5. In the past, the king often had to abstain from the precepts for three days for sacrifice and then discuss the battle plan with the generals at the temple before raising soldiers.

Chapter 2 – Combating 作戰

1. The army here consisted of a hundred thousand soldiers divided into one thousand battalions. Each battalion has one hundred soldiers and is provided with a light chariot wagon and a heavy chariot wagon.

2. A light chariot wagon consists of four fast-moving horses, usually used for attacks. Each light chariot wagon has 75 soldiers to follow.

3. The heavy chariot wagons are often used for defense. Each heavy chariot wagon has 25 soldiers.

4. Ancient armor was usually made of bamboo or animal skin.

5. Li 英里: 1 li = 0.5789 km.

6. During this time, about 400 - 500 BC, people used gold to trade or exchange, not money currency.

7. In the old days people used the word "hundred people" as a number to generally refer to all people in the country, not just one hundred of them in a country.

8. 1 bushel = 40 liters. An old unit of volume measurement.

9. 1 picul of fodder 一 匹 草 = 50 kg. An old unit of weight measurement.

Chapter 3 – Offensive Strategy 謀攻

1. The word army 師 here meant one division is consisting of 12500 soldiers.

2. One brigade consists of 500 soldiers.

3. One regiment consists of 100 soldiers.

4. One battalion consists of 5 soldiers.

5. Attack the strategic plan of the enemy.

6. Prevent the coalition forces to create more military power for the enemy.

7. Use your military strength to fight.

8. It means fighting at the enemy strong fortifications.

9. For example, making special moving vehicles so soldiers can hide inside while getting close to enemy wall gates.

10. The high mounds for observing enemy movement in the city or for our soldiers to jump over enemy walls and attack.

11. If our army is five times the size of the enemy, we can make enemy pays attention to the front, surprise him in rear, create a stir in the east and attack the west.

12. It is possible to use the tactic of deploying a few of our troops in the east but attacking in the west.

13. Reduce enemy military power.

Chapter 4 – Military Disposition 軍形

1. This vulnerability may be due to lack of preparation, lack of stratagem. Here, I think Sun Vu referred to weather created by nature such as heavy rain, dry weather, dark clouds etc., so people are not in control to plan ahead. Our general Trần Hưng Đạo was very good at this subject, he taught the technique of considering the appearance of stars to accurately forecast weather conditioning in advance in the first part of his book called "The Essential Art of War". But most of our translators did not translate that part because they thought it was vague.

2. In acient Chinese, they believed the earth's gods lived under nine layer of the earth. One of eight gods belongs to the eight trigrams. It is believed that anyone who enters under the ninth layers is easy to hide and defend because this layer is the deepest.

3. Same as above, Chinese people believed there were nine levels of heaven. The nineth layer is supposed to be highest, therefore it is easier to attack if one is staying in this layer. We may think now as using aircrafts to attack ground.

4. Defeating the enemy is very easy because the great general had previously created situations for the enemy to be in a defeated position.

5. 1 "dật" = 500 grams.

6. 1 "thù" = 1 gram.

7. 1 "knobstick" = 6.48 meters.

Chapter 5 – Military Force 兵勢

1. "Indirect" here means attacking enemy force on the side (left or right). Usually, it is a surprise attack using strange moves that the enemy has not thought of.

2. "Direct" here means attacking enemy force head on.

3. The magic of real and unreal is to make enemy confuse of what is real and what is fake from us. Mainly for enemy not able to predict our true intentions.

4. The five based colors are red, blue, yellow, white, and black.

5. The five based flavors are sour, bitter, salty, sweet, and spicy.

Chapter 6 – Real and Unreal 虛 實

1. Five elements are metal, wood, water, fire, and earth.

2. Four seasons are spring, summer, autumn, and winter.

Chapter 7 – Maneuvering 軍 爭

1. The three generals here meant the general holding three troops is the commander in chief of the front, middle and rear battle troops.

2. Here means the front, middle, and rear enemy troops.

Chapter 8 – Nine Changes 九 變

1. Barren land is the place where food and water supplies are scarce.

2. Being surrounded with no way out.

3. In a very dangerous situation, if one doesn't fight back with all ones has, he will die for sure. Fighting back may have a chance to survive.

4. Because there are roads if passing by will destroy your troops.

5. If we are not sure we will win, we will not fight.

6. Besiege the fortresses take times and risk of not taking it.

7. The terrain is not favorable, we do not fight.

8. If according to the king's order we will lose the battle, then we should not follow.

9. I am guessing the five benefits that Sun Vu mentioned here are from the 1st chapter on Planning: righteousness, atmosphere, terrain, general, and martial law.

Chapter 9 – Marching 行 軍

1. Relying on the stream has the advantage of having a source of drinking water for soldiers.

2. It is difficult for soldiers to fighting up because the earth's gravity always pulled down soldiers' weight and weapons. Soldiers have to use more strength to both advance and fight.

3. On contrary, fighting down is easy and takes less effort, especially in the past, soldiers often use spears to fight.

4. The enemy's soldiers in the middle of stream will be in turmoil and can't do much. If the force is the same then it's two against one, we can see that we have double advantage.

5. Same principle as 'Don't climb up to join battle on high ground.'

6. Because it's difficult to move and easy to get ambush. Beside, human don't drink salt water.

7. It is not clear who king Huỳnh Đế is but the old books noted that king Si Vưu of Viêm Việt used the four topographical tactics in this chapter to defeat all four neighbor kings, including Tam Miêu.

8. Because the fear of sudden water rise, the troops will be drown or separate and could not save each other in this situation.

9.   The enemy is thristy.

Chapter 10 – Terrain 地 形

1.   Usually southeast.

2.   Exit is difficult because rivers, trenches or strongholds. So it's easy to be surrounded by enemy when withdraw troops.

3.   The army entering this terrain is difficult to battle due to the lack of force concentration because of dividing forces.

4.   This terrains usually have cliffs on both side and very narrow path in the middle.

5.   These terrains are usually pass, bar, hill, mountain, abyss etc. Attack here is easy to trap death.

6.   Because it is far and wide, it is difficult to supply weapons, food, and reinforcements.

7.   In the past, incompetent kings and general often blame 'heaven and earth' for their mistake.

8.   Run before the fight.

9.   Run after lost battle.

10. In the past, if general lose a battle, he often get humiliated and guilty before his king.

Chapter 11 – Nine Ground Positions 九 地

1.   The position to against enemy on dipersed ground is to fight enemy on the lands within one's own country. Therefore soldiers often linger on wife, children, brothers, sisters, and parents. That is why they are easily flee or not risk death against enemy. So they are often broken or failed.

2. On shoal ground, the soldiers are often depressed, wanting to retreat back to their homeland.

3. In a position to compete with the enemy to gain advantage.

4. Hưng Đạo Vương Trần Quốc Tuấn used this tactic perfectly against the Mongols in the 13th century. He didn't directly attack where the Mongols wanted but keep the important grounds for later suprise attack. He made sure the enemy can't get any food supplies from our land while destroyed enemy food supplies. At first, he didn't engage in battle on our land to peiserved the vigor of the army and people. He waited for enemy to be in mysterious then total attack and win in the end.

5. Camping and linger on shoal ground has many disadvantages. Our soldiers' moral is in a situation of fatique, fear and fustration.

6. Because one doesn't want to lose our troops when enemy prepared. But if one takes it first, there are many advantages.

7. When going deep into enemy territory, food for troops is one of the most critical jobs because it is difficult, expensive and dangerous to transport from thousands of miles.

8. Forest mountains, rugged cliffs, swamps and wetlands are difficult to move as well as reinforcements but easy to be destroyed by ambushes so we must quickly move out of these places.

9. Being surrounded on all sides, it is impossible to use ordinary tactics to break the siege.

10. On death ground, if one decides to fight hard then one might survive and win, but not if he has no chance to survive.

11. Taking the most advantageous conditions of the enemy in advance, it is imperative that he has to change from being active

to passive. The enemy was in a passive position, so he had to follow your control.

12. Legend has it that Chuyên Chư was from Wu country, hid a small sword in grilled fish's belly, stabbed Vương Liễu, Wu's prince, to repay prince Quang for nuturing and taking care of Chuyên Chư old mother. Chuyên Chư was killed by Vương Liễu bodyguards. Thanks to that, prince Quang was crowned king, namely Hạp Lư of the Wu dynasty.

13. Tào Quế is high official from Lỗ dynasty. When Tề Hoàn Công met his vassals in Khá territory, Tào Quế held a sword to inhibit Tề Hoàn Công asking him to repay Lỗ territory.

14. Today people do not know for sure what kind of snake is Suất Thiên in the mountain of Hoành Sơn. But in 'bát trận' said that sometimes 'trận xà bàn' can change to 'Suất Thiên' formation.

Chapter 12 – Fire Attack 火攻

1. According to lunar calendar, these four days are 7, 14, 27, and 28.

2. Quickly attack from the outside to help our troops in the enemy camp and win.

3. Do not attack immediately because enemy may have prepared.

4. The principle of fire is to burn according to the wind direction. One doesn't want to attack against wind direction because it will burn one's troops. In contrast, attacking with wind direction is to use the wind to burn one's enemy.

Chapter 13 – Using Spy 用間

1. One 'vạn' = 10000. This is the unit for measuring quantity. Sun Vu wrote 10 vạn so it is 100000 soldiers.

2. The national public fund here is understood as the court (kingdom) members (king family and its relatives). These people must contribute money, armors, weapons, horses, food etc. to the war.

3. During Sun Vu time, the court (kingdom) divided land as follow: 8 houses were entitled to own 9 plots of land. The middle space is used to build houses and dig wells. Each house is given a space around for cultivation and plowing. If any house has a soldier, the other seven houses must provide all expenses such as clothing as well as laborious service to follow to carry the transport. That is why 100,000 soldiers bothered 700,000 houses.

4. In the past, kings and generals used to believe in superstition.

5. Local people knows about their place of living more accurate than foreigners. The issue is whether they accept the work for the other party or not. Often the local spies are lured to work for other party.

6. The officials were dissatisfied with the court or had their own personal gain.

7. These types of spies are often bribed by means or known to be enemy spies, but we pretend to be ignorant and reveal false information so they can misreport us.

8. The suicide spy is our spy against enemy's spy. So when enemy sees things that don't happen right, they will kill that person. Therefore, it should be called suicide.

9. The report spy is our spy lying in the heart of enemy. He is intelligent, high position, and influential person. He scanned the enemy's military openly without fear of being exposed.

10. Y Doãn was the general of the Ân dynasty.

11. Khương Tử Nha was the chief strategist advisor for Zhou dynasty.

www.ingramcontent.com/pod-product-compliance
Lightning Source LLC
Chambersburg PA
CBHW021800190326
41518CB00007B/382